# R.E.S.U.L.T.S.

Promoting Positive Behavior and Responsibility for Learning

**Krista M. Venza and Jonathan R. Treese**

## EduGladiators

Book Design & Production: Columbus Publishing Lab
www.ColumbusPublishingLab.com

Copyright © 2019 by EduGladiators
www.edugladiators.com

All rights reserved. This book, or parts thereof, may not be reproduced in any form without permission.

LCCN: 2019931995
Paperback ISBN: 978-1-7336864-0-2
E-book ISBN: 978-1-7336864-1-9

Printed in the United States of America
1 3 5 7 9 10 8 6 4 2

# Praise for R.E.S.U.L.T.S.

"R.E.S.U.L.T.S. is a book that all school administrators need to read and put into practice at their schools. Krista and Jonathan are tackling a long-standing issue, how to support students that act out and best support them in the school environment. With great stories and practical tips for implementation, they really hit a home run and I know this book will benefit schools all across the country."

—Adam Welcome, author, speaker, keynote speaker,
co-founder of Kids Deserve It, marathon runner, principal of the year,
Ed Week blogger, NSBA 20 To Watch
Lafayette, CA, adamwelcome@gmail.com

"Working toward pro-social growth with students can be the most rewarding of times as well as the most challenging. While Krista Venza and Jon Treese acknowledge that there is no 'magic behavior wand,' this book provides a positive framework that is rooted in the principles of behavior modification. Anyone who works with students can benefit from taking the time to dive deeper into R.E.S.U.L.T.S. Thank you, Krista and Jon, from all the students who will find that caring individual who was inspired by reading this book."

—Zach Milch M Ed., licensed behavior specialist
Reading, PA, milchz@muhlsdk12.org

"Any adult working with children would benefit from this book. Not only do Krista and Jon describe practical strategies for supporting students with challenging behaviors, they also share stories of success in a real way. This book takes a more restorative approach to helping students create solutions within their own lives. This creative, out-of-the-box thinking, provides a positive approach to help all students. Krista and Jon are rock stars who need to be cloned so they can be a part of every teacher preparation program across the country!"

—Kira Marks, 7th grade learning support teacher
Pottstown, PA, kmarks@ojrsd.com

"*R.E.S.U.L.T.S.* is a book designed to help every educator identify behaviors and it will walk you through ways to make connections with students and truly get the RESULTS desired by every school. Krista and Jon use stories and their own experiences to engage readers and provide practical advice that every educator can implement tomorrow. I highly recommend this read for any educator who wants to make a difference in a child's life."

—Ryan Sheehy, principal, speaker,
author of *Be The One For Kids: You Have The Power To Change The Life Of A Child*
Concord, CA, mrryansheehy@gmail.com

"In *R.E.S.U.L.T.S.*, Krista and Jon have put together a process that can be adapted and used in your school today. The process is not just meant to improve behavior, which it does, but it has aspects which work to improve academics and goal setting. At the center of the process is the relationship that is built between student and educator. The forms and anecdotes that are shared by Krista and Jon help bring this process to life. If you are an educator at any level, *R.E.S.U.L.T.S.* is a book that can help you connect with all of your students and guide them toward success."

—Jay Posick, principal
Hartland, WI, jayposick@gmail.com

"In *R.E.S.U.L.T.S.*, Krista Venza and Jon Treese provide a framework and mindset that can be applied to academic and behavioral work with students at all levels. The authors are strong advocates for creating positive relationships and being proactive so students and educators can achieve success. You'll be glad you added this resource to your toolbox."

—Mark French, principal,
past president of the Minnesota Elementary School Principals' Association,
2015 Minnesota National Distinguished Principal
Golden Valley, MN, drmarkfrench@gmail.com

"My first experience with Krista & Jon's R.E.S.U.L.T.S framework was during a conference with everyone on the edge of their seats during their presentation. If you are searching for a proactive behavior process that prioritizes the needs of kids with practical implementation strategies, look no further. This book is packed with best practices you can use today with your students."

—Marlena Gross-Taylor, founder of EduGladiators

*This book is dedicated to all of the incredible educators we work with who strive to make a difference in the lives of their students each and every day.*

*To all of our students, thank you for reminding us of the importance of making connections and never giving up.*

*At the end of the book, you will hear from one of our former students, Samantha, who has touched our hearts in profound ways. We are in awe of her hard work, drive, and resilient spirit.*

*Special thanks to:*
*Marlena Gross-Taylor*
*Jonathan Wennstrom*
*Adam Welcome*
*Mark French*
*Jay Posick*
*Ryan Sheehy*
*Kira Marks*
*Zach Milch*
*Samantha R.*
*A.J.*

Additional resources and full-size versions of the forms that appear throughout R.E.S.U.L.T.S. are available by scanning the QR code below. The authors hope these materials are useful in your classroom and beyond.

# CONTENTS

| | |
|---|---|
| **Foreword** | 9 |
| **Introduction** | 11 |
| **1** R.E.S.U.L.T.S. | 14 |
| **2** Let's Break It Down | 21 |
| **3** Recognizing the Function of Student Behavior | 50 |
| **4** Connections | 56 |
| **5** Is What's Good for Us Good for Our Students? | 62 |
| **6** Explicitly Teaching Skills | 67 |
| **7** Consequences vs. Learning Opportunities | 70 |
| **8** Make Detention and In-School Suspension Learning Opportunities | 75 |
| **9** Reinforcing Behaviors | 85 |
| **10** Meeting Social and Emotional Needs | 89 |
| **11** Applying R.E.S.U.L.T.S. in the Classroom | 95 |
| **12** Focus on Growth | 103 |
| **13** Family Buy-In and Support | 109 |
| **14** Self-Care and Emotional Wellness for Staff | 112 |
| **15** Final Thoughts | 116 |
| **About the Authors** | 119 |
| **Special Thanks** | 122 |

# Foreword
## Jonathon Wennstrom

I've always been a fan of the Albert Einstein quote: "The definition of insanity is doing the same thing over and over again and expecting a different result." As a school leader, I have often been confronted with behavior issues, and like the example in Einstein's quote, I have often repeated the standard methods of dealing with the behaviors that are focused on short-term consequences rather than long-term changes. Good intentions that don't yield lasting results. As I read R.E.S.U.L.T.S. by Krista Venza and Jonathan Treese, I quickly realized that this book wasn't about managing behaviors, it was about getting to the root of the problem and creating a culture that is proactive rather than reactive. They provide practical and realistic strategies for lasting changes by helping students learn responsibility for their actions and by helping teachers learn ways to support students through explicit teaching of desired behaviors. In short, they provide a road map for ways to break the cycle of negative behavior that often exists in the school setting, while supporting students with academics at the same time.

While many parts of the book speak to the head as the authors give practical advice and helpful charts and guides, many parts of the book speak to the heart as well. They emphasize the importance of believing in students, in having a positive voice with parents, and the necessity of self-care for teachers. The book starts and ends with an emphasis on the need for strong relationships and knowing your students. Realizing that all behavior is need driven, we first need to understand the needs of our students before we can help them. Many strategies are given to help identify those needs, and ways are provided to assist in asking our students what they need both socially and academically.

The philosophy and strategies found in this book are not only beneficial to struggling students, but to all students. That is why this book focuses on culture as well as practice. Not forgetting the voices that are most important, the book ends with a testimonial from a student sharing the difference a caring and thoughtful approach made in her life, which is echoed by Krista and Jon's reminder that we are not just educators, but life changers!

If you are looking for a quick fix or Band-Aid approach to behavior issues, you will not find it here. This book shares ways to help create a culture where traditional consequences are replaced with learning opportunities, where behavior expectations are explicitly taught and where relationships are developed with even our most challenging students. These strategies take time, effort, and a team approach—just like all the worthwhile things in life. I hope you enjoy this book as much as I did.

Jonathon Wennstrom<br>Elementary Principal

Jon is a principal for Livonia Public Schools in the Metro Detroit area. He has twenty-four years of experience in education ranging from classroom teacher, high school wrestling coach, theater director, chief academic officer, online instructor, and his current and favorite position, elementary school principal. Outside of school, he is a member of Rotary International, and is the president-elect for the Michigan Elementary & Middle School Principals Association (MEMSPA). Most recently, he was named the 2018 Michigan PTA administrator of the year.

You can follow Jon on Twitter @jon_wennstrom<br>and read his weekly blog posts on leadership and education at<br>www.jonwennstrom.com (The Spark of Learning).

# Introduction

We do not know about you, but we've never had students thank us for making a difference in their lives by assigning them their fifth detention or suspending them. Throwing discipline at a behavior does not fix the behavior. Actually, many times it increases the disruption caused by students struggling to meet expectations. Relationships, engaging instruction, explicitly taught expectations, and opportunities to practice are what change behaviors . . . and therefore change lives.

> *Throwing discipline at a behavior does not fix the behavior.*

For three years we worked together in a middle school as the assistant principal and dean of students. We quickly realized that we share the same passion for making a difference in the lives of our students as well as the same belief that school should be much more than the curriculum and instruction of academics. We are interested in creating opportunities to grow and support students academically, but more importantly as thinkers, doers, and creators—and in general into good human beings who positively contribute to the community and, ultimately, the world.

In our roles as the people who primarily dealt with disciplinary issues, we found that removing students from classrooms and assigning traditional consequences were not answers for changing behavior. Does this action temporarily remove a challenging student and give the teacher and class a break? Yes, but the same student eventually goes back to the same classroom with the same problem behaviors. And so the cycle continues over and over because we are not addressing the reason why the student is acting out.

We understand that discipline policies and consequences exist, and many people in and outside of education feel that discipline needs to be assigned. To an extent, we absolutely agree. We get it. It is really difficult to teach when a student is acting out, not cooperating, or constantly disrupting others. This is not okay, and it should not be allowed to happen. Where we get hung up with traditional consequences is that they typically don't address the problem.

Traditional consequences do not seek out the root cause of behavior. It usually looks like a kid sitting in detention or in-school suspension feeling bored, miserable, and angry. This turns into more acting out and struggling to meet expectations. In essence, this makes discipline a big waste of time for everyone.

When we see kids act out, it is usually because of any combination of the following reasons: students do not know the expectations, weren't given enough opportunities to practice the expectations, and/or haven't met with enough success when following the expectations. Once students meet with success in following expectations, they will be able to recognize that it feels better than acting out, and they will receive more positive attention for making good choices. Addressing these issues along with forming relationships with supportive adults is the key to changing behaviors.

The R.E.S.U.L.T.S. framework takes into account the necessity for holding students accountable through disciplinary consequences. We identify the "time"

> *... forming relationships with supportive adults is the key to changing behaviors.*

of the consequence assigned as the discipline, but what we do during that time is what changes behavior. The R.E.S.U.L.T.S. framework systematically lays out learning opportunities and supports for varying levels of behaviors.

In addition, we have all witnessed the "Catch-22" of problem behaviors and academic success. Students who are not academically successful often act out in class. This acting out causes students to miss instruction and fall behind. They dig themselves a hole that becomes so deep they cannot see over the edge and don't know how to climb out on their own. This is where we see frequency and severity of behaviors increase because students are experiencing failure in all areas of school.

There is no perfect prescription of strategies and interventions that work all of the time for every student. This is why it is imperative that every student has a connection with a trusted adult in the school who will never give up on them. This person will play a key role in working on the root of the problem and creating success for the student.

Throughout this book we will share situations we have encountered with students, how we handled them, and sometimes how we wish we had handled them. Our framework promotes positive behavior, taking responsibility for learning, and getting RESULTS!

# CHAPTER ONE
# R.E.S.U.L.T.S.

## KRISTA

Several years ago, while serving as the instructional support facilitator in a different middle school, I developed a program to help students who struggled with work completion and passing their classes. I called the program R.E.S.U.L.T.S. Students attended R.E.S.U.L.T.S. during their team time and lunch period, which were back-to-back and provided an hour of work time. I ran a grade report the day before each R.E.S.U.L.T.S. session, students were given passes during their first period class, and it was mandatory for them to attend. The students brought their lunches to the session, and I tried to glamorize it by calling it a "working lunch."

Each letter of R.E.S.U.L.T.S. stood for an action that the students were to complete during the session, such as reviewing their grades, evaluating their progress, or studying. The students completed a form where they recorded their grades, made a list of the assignments they owed, and set a goal for the upcoming week. This program ran twice a week and successfully helped many students complete work, organize their materials, and pass their classes.

When I moved into administration as an assistant principal, my focus shifted from being solely on instruction to addressing behaviors as well. I quickly noticed I was seeing the same students repeatedly for disruptive behaviors. It did not take long to realize that the traditional menu of discipline that I had available to me was not working.

At the end of my first year as assistant principal, Jon's position as in-school suspension teacher was changed to the role of dean of students. I certainly welcomed the assistance addressing behaviors, but it became apparent that the only difference was that now there were two of us going through the same motions—assigning ineffective discipline.

We found ourselves trying everything we could think of to support the same "revolving door" of students engaging in the same disruptive behaviors. We met with kids about grades, stopped them in the halls just to say hello, went to their classrooms, checked in with their teachers, contacted home, called them down to our offices, and created an after-school service club and a summer leadership academy. This took up a huge amount of time, but we needed to figure out a way to help our kids because we knew that assigning yet another detention was not going to bring about change.

Let's talk about traditional discipline. Typically, detention is an hour after school and is supervised by someone who spends the time planning or grading. The rules for detention are usually as follows: sit at a desk, don't talk, and don't sleep. There is probably an expectation that students should do some kind of work, but this may be overlooked as long as they are quiet.

Many students who end up in detention struggle to follow expectations. Then add in being bored, angry about having to be there, and possibly feeling like they need to put on a show, and a recipe for disaster has been created. We all know what happens: kids talk, they do not listen to the monitor, the monitor gets frustrated and calls for an administrator, yelling usually takes place . . . This is not a productive or pleasant situation for anyone, and most importantly, nothing happens to help change behavior.

In-school suspension (ISS) is more of the same, but it is All. Day. Long! Some schools have a designated ISS monitor so at least there is consistency. When Jon's position changed to dean of students, we lost the ISS teacher position and needed to pull a different person to cover ISS each class period. This allowed us to run ISS, but it was difficult for students because, although there were rules for ISS, everyone who covered had a different interpretation of the expectations and the behaviors that should be tolerated.

Many schools do not have expectations that the ISS monitor will interact with students in a restorative way. ISS simply becomes a punishment where little academic or restorative learning takes place. Unfortunately, some students end up being assigned out-of-school suspension because they simply cannot manage to make it through the day, often for the same reasons they were assigned ISS in the first place.

Jon and I spent hours talking about ideas, strategies, and behavioral interventions, and we always came back to the need to explicitly teach students expectations, give them the opportunity to practice, and provide support so that they met with success. It was also clear that finding a strategy that worked was not the only factor that led to success. It is critical for students to have an adult in the school whom they trust and have a connection with.

> *It is critical for students to have an adult in the school whom they trust and have a connection with.*

Many students met with success because they grew to trust us, even if we were not always their favorite people. They knew that we cared and were not going to give up on them and were going to keep coming back to support them no matter how many times they pushed us away. Making connections and building relationships is the secret sauce to this recipe!

Jon and I and a committed group of teachers with fantastic ideas and a lot of creativity spent the next two summers developing our Positive Behavior Support framework for our school. We rolled out the framework to the whole staff and spent a portion of the first week of school teaching our school's nonnegotiables, explicitly teaching expectations, and making connections with our kids. Our plan was to frontload all of this great stuff and then give "booster shots" along the way throughout the school year. We figured that we would spend time, one way or another, addressing these things, so it would be prudent for us to do it all together at the start of the year in order to set the tone and create a great environment for teaching and learning.

We presented the nonnegotiables in a matrix describing what each nonnegotiable looked like in every area of our school, including the classrooms, hallways, cafeteria, auditorium, restrooms, buses, and during extra-curricular activities. We then discussed, practiced, and engaged in activities that supported what the nonnegotiables looked like, sounded like, and felt like in different scenarios and locations.

### Nonnegotiables

✓ Treat everyone with respect and kindness. Everyone. No exceptions.

✓ Take responsibility for our learning and set high expectations for ourselves. Everyone. No exceptions.

✓ Show pride in ourselves and our school. Everyone. No exceptions.

The presentations, information, activities, and materials were supplied to the teachers so that everyone was communicating the same message. It was also important to us that this was not something the teachers had to plan for. We wanted the teachers to focus on getting to know their kids, forming relationships, and delivering the information in the most enthusiastic, rock-star way possible!

This plan successfully supports most students, but have you ever heard people say that 5–7 percent of your population takes up 90 percent of your time? This is what we find to be true. A small percentage of students continue to struggle even after all of the frontloading. They need more explicit instruction and practice.

Getting back to disciplinary consequences—they exist in public education and are expected to be enforced. Therefore, the students who fall into the 5–7 percent category end up being assigned lunch detentions, after-school detentions, in-school suspension, and even out-of-school suspension. We know that it is important to a lot of people that students receive consequences and are held accountable. We agree, but will forever maintain that assigning these consequences alone will not change behaviors.

We merge these two philosophies, the need to have students serve consequences with the need to explicitly teach expectations, practice them, and make connections. We look at the consequence of the "time" they serve as the discipline.

Knowing this, however, is not enough to change behaviors. We attended conferences, read books, researched programs, talked with other educators, and had many conversations about what we could do to address what was lacking in traditional disciplinary consequences. Then we decided to revamp the original academic R.E.S.U.L.T.S. program and added a behavioral component to the framework. We changed some of the tasks so that they would address both academics and behaviors to promote positive behavior and responsibility for learning.

In Chapter 2 we will provide an in-depth look at each of the tasks as well as resources to use to guide students through reflective activities, opportunities that allow for practice, and tools students may use to maintain the skills they have learned.

| At our school we: | Classroom | Hallway | Cafeteria |
|---|---|---|---|
| Treat everyone with respect and kindness. Everyone. No exceptions. | • Use "school language" priate volume, respectful tone and word choice) <br> • Acknowledge others <br> • Listen to others <br> • Exhibit positive manners (say please and thank you) and body language <br> • Provide positive support toward others <br> • Keep hands and feet to yourself | • Use "school language" priate volume, respectful tone and word choice) so as not to disrupt classes <br> • Stop and listen when spoken to by adults <br> • Use problem-solving strategies <br> • Be aware of others and your surroundings <br> • Be respectful of others' personal space <br> • Keep your hands and feet to yourself | • Use "school language" priate volume, respectful tone and word choice) <br> • Exhibit positive manners (say please and thank you) and body language <br> • Wait patiently in line <br> • Use problem-solving strategies <br> • Stop and listen when spoken to by adults <br> • Keep your hands and feet to yourself |
| Take responsibility for our learning and set high expectations for ourselves. Everyone. No exceptions. | • Be on time for school and class <br> • Bring assignments and materials <br> • Be organized <br> • Be seated and ready to participate <br> • Follow classroom procedures <br> • Keep electronics off and put away in your locker unless directed by a teacher <br> • Be alert and awake <br> • Participate in activities <br> • Complete all assignments <br> • Ask for help when needed <br> • Check grades weekly <br> • Keep parents and guardians informed <br> • Wear your school ID at all times <br> • Carry and use your planner for assignments and as your hall pass | • Walk at all times <br> • Walk on the right side of the hallway <br> • Report only to assigned area <br> • Take shortest, most direct route to assigned area <br> • Follow sign out/in procedures <br> • Use only your assigned locker and keep your combination private <br> • Wear your school ID at all times <br> • Carry and use your planner for assignments and as your hall pass | • Be on time <br> • Keep electronics off and put away in your locker <br> • Clean up your table and floor <br> • Stay in your seat until your table is dismissed by an adult <br> • Follow cafeteria procedures <br> • Follow sign out/in procedures <br> • Follow first 2/last 2 minute rule <br> • Wear your school ID at all times |
| Show pride in ourselves and our school. Everyone. No exceptions. | • Follow the dress code <br> • Be a positive role model <br> • Complete work neatly and on time <br> • Give your best effort <br> • Participate in team and school activities <br> • Keep classroom neat <br> • Keep food and drink out of the classroom <br> • Respect school and others' personal property | • Follow the dress code <br> • Report any problems, concerns or unsafe situations to an adult <br> • Pick up after yourself and throw away trash <br> • Keep food and drink out of the hallway <br> • Respect school and others' personal property | • Follow the dress code <br> • Report any problems, concerns or unsafe situations to an adult <br> • Clean up after yourself <br> • Pick up after yourself and throw away trash <br> • Respect school and others' personal property |

# R.E.S.U.L.T.S.

| Auditorium | Restroom | Bus | Extra-Curricular |
|---|---|---|---|
| • Use "school language" (appropriate volume, respectful tone and word choice)<br>• Exhibit positive manners and body language<br>• Pay close attention to the performer(s) and speaker(s)<br>• Applaud politely at appropriate times<br>• Stop and listen when spoken to by adults<br>• Keep hands and feet to yourself | • Use "school language" (appropriate volume, respectful tone and word choice)<br>• Honor the privacy of others<br>• Use problem-solving strategies<br>• Keep your hands and feet to yourself | • Use "school language" (appropriate volume, respectful tone and word choice)<br>• Use problem-solving strategies<br>• Exhibit positive manners (say please and thank you) and body language<br>• Stop and listen when spoken to by driver/adults<br>• Keep hands and feet to yourself | • Use "school language" (appropriate volume, respectful tone and word choice)<br>• Exhibit positive manners and body language<br>• Provide positive support toward others<br>• Cheer and applaud at appropriate times<br>• Respect the judgment of officials<br>• Show respect for opposing teams<br>• Stop and listen when spoken to by adults<br>• Keep hands and feet to yourself |
| **Before School**<br>When entering the building...<br>• Dispose of or put away food or drinks<br>• Remove hats/hoods<br>• Turn off and put electronics away<br>• Find a seat and remain seated until dismissed<br><br>**Dismissal**<br>• Sit in your designated bus section<br>• Stay seated until your section is called<br>• Keep electronic devices away until you exit the building<br><br>**Assembly**<br>• Walk quietly with your homebase and stay with your teacher<br>• Sit in your homebase's assigned section<br>• Sit up in your seat<br>• Be alert and awake | • Follow sign out/in procedures<br>• Use restroom at designated times<br>• Use restroom closest to where you are coming from<br>• Return directly to your designated location (go, flush, wash, leave)<br>• Wear your school ID at all times | • Be on time for your pick up and dismissal<br>• Board the bus promptly<br>• Sit in assigned seat if applicable | • Sit in designated spectator locations when attending sporting events and performances<br>• Encourage those around you to display sportsmanlike conduct at sporting events<br>• Be picked up on time after events are over |
| • Follow the dress code<br>• Report any problems, concerns or unsafe situations to an adult<br>• Clean up after yourself<br>• Keep food and drink out of the auditorium | • Follow the dress code<br>• Report any problems, concerns or unsafe situations to an adult<br>• Dispose of trash appropriately<br>• Respect school and others' personal property | • Follow the dress code<br>• Report any problems, concerns or unsafe situations to an adult<br>• Clean up after yourself<br>• Keep food and drink away until you exit the bus | • Report any problems, concerns or unsafe situations to an adult<br>• Clean up after yourself<br>• Keep food and drink out of auditoriums<br>• Cheer on our teams<br>• Be a positive role model through your actions |

## CHAPTER TWO
# Let's Break it Down

### KRISTA

When referring to the R.E.S.U.L.T.S. framework, we address student behavior with the term "choices and consequences" and academics with the term "Learning."

> ### R.E.S.U.L.T.S.
> #### Promoting Positive Behavior and Responsibility for Learning
>
> **R - Review your current situation**
> E - Evaluate your progress
> S - Self-assess
> U - Utilize time wisely
> L - Lose the clutter
> T - Take initiative
> S - Set goals

#### R – Review Your Current Situation

- Choices and Actions

# R.E.S.U.L.T.S.

- What happened? Why was I assigned a consequence?
  - Have the student state the facts from his or her perspective. The student should speak or write about the situation that resulted in the disciplinary consequence.
  - R.E.S.U.L.T.S.: Review Your Current Behavioral Situation Worksheet

---

**R.E.S.U.L.T.S.**
**Review Your Current Behavioral Situation – Choices and Actions**

Name _____     Date _____

What happened? Describe what happened and the current situation from your perspective.




---

| Reviewed with | Next steps |
|---|---|
|  |  |

- Learning
    - What are my grades in each of my classes? Am I missing any assignments?
        - The student should record his or her grades and list any missing assignments.
        - R.E.S.U.L.T.S.: Review Your Current Academic Situation Worksheet

### R.E.S.U.L.T.S.
#### Review Your Current Academic Situation

Name _____ Date _____ Team _____ Homeroom _____

| Class | Teacher | Grade | Missing Assignment(s) |
|---|---|---|---|
| ELA | | | |
| Math | | | |
| Science | | | |
| Social Studies | | | |
| | | | |

| Reviewed with | Next steps |
|---|---|
| | |

> **R.E.S.U.L.T.S.**
> **Promoting Positive Behavior and Responsibility for Learning**
>
> R - Review your current situation
> **E - Evaluate your progress**
> S - Self-assess
> U - Utilize time wisely
> L - Lose the clutter
> T - Take initiative
> S - Set goals

### E – Evaluate Your Progress

- Choices and Actions
    - What is triggering these behaviors?
        - The student should list or discuss what he or she feels is causing him or her to engage in the problem behavior.
        - Evaluate Your Progress — Choices and Actions Form

## R.E.S.U.L.T.S.
### Evaluate Your Progress – Choices and Actions

Name _____          Date_____

What triggered the choices and actions of concern? What event, situation, or person contributed to your choices and actions?




Did you recognize or feel this trigger affecting you before you engaged in the behavior of concern? If so, describe what you felt. What happened to you mentally, physically, and/or emotionally?




| Reviewed with | Next steps |
|---|---|
|  |  |

R.E.S.U.L.T.S.

- Learning
    - What is standing in my way of being successful?
        - The student should list or discuss what he or she feels is preventing him or her from being successful academically.
        - Evaluate Your Progress — Learning Form

---

**R.E.S.U.L.T.S.**
**Evaluate Your Progress – Learning**

Name _____     Date_____

What is holding you back from being successful academically?




Reflect on a time when you chose to do something else (play video games, text, go on social media) instead of doing something that would help you to be more successful academically (study your notes, read a chapter, complete homework). Discuss why you made that decision.

---

| Reviewed with | Next steps |
|---|---|
|  |  |

> # R.E.S.U.L.T.S.
> ## Promoting Positive Behavior and Responsibility for Learning
>
> R - Review your current situation
> E - Evaluate your progress
> **S - Self-assess**
> U - Utilize time wisely
> L - Lose the clutter
> T - Take initiative
> S - Set goals

### S – Self-Assess

- Choices and Actions
    - How did my choice(s) impact me? How did my choice(s) impact others? What will I do to make the situation better for myself? What will I do to mend the relationship(s) that were affected? If physical damage to property occurred, what can I do to make restitution or fix the damaged property?
        - The student may need guidance in recognizing how his or her choice makes a negative impact on his or her life, as well as how it impacts others.
        - Self-Assessment — Choices and Actions Form

R.E.S.U.L.T.S.

**R.E.S.U.L.T.S.**
**Self-Assess Your Behavior – Choices and Actions**

Name _____          Date_____

How did my action(s) impact me?

How did my action(s) impact others?

What can I do to make the situation better for myself?

What can I do to mend the relationship(s) that were affected by my action(s)? If damage to property occurred, what can I do to make restitution or fix the damaged property?

| Reviewed with | Next steps |
|---|---|
|  |  |

- Learning
    - How have my choice(s) impacted my academics? How could my choice(s) impact my future options? What can I do to fix the negative impact my choices have made on my academics?
        - The student may need guidance in recognizing how his or her choices and/or lack of effort may limit future life choices.
        - Self-Assess — Learning Form

---

**R.E.S.U.L.T.S.**
**Self-Assess – Learning**

Name _____     Date_____

How have my action(s) impacted my learning?



How could my action(s) negatively impact my future options?



What can I do to fix the negative impact my choices have made on my academics?

---

| Reviewed with | Next steps |
|---|---|
|  |  |

> **R.E.S.U.L.T.S.**
> **Promoting Positive Behavior and Responsibility for Learning**
>
> R - Review your current situation
> E - Evaluate your progress
> S - Self-assess
> **U - Utilize time wisely**
> L - Lose the clutter
> T - Take initiative
> S - Set goals

### U – Utilize Time Wisely

- Choices and Actions
    - How can I use my time to develop positive behaviors? What area(s) do I need to focus my time working on?
        - The student should be explicitly taught and given opportunities to practice strategies to proactively avoid making poor choices and engaging in negative behaviors. The student may benefit from being taught meditation, stop-and-think strategies, breathing exercises, yoga, or how to properly ask for a break and/or excuse him- or herself from a situation.
        - Utilize Time Wisely — Choices and Actions Form

## R.E.S.U.L.T.S.
### Utilize Time Wisely – Choices and Actions

Name _____       Date_____

How can I use my time to develop positive behaviors? What area(s) do I need to focus my time working on?

| Reviewed with | Next steps |
|---|---|
|  |  |

# R.E.S.U.L.T.S.

- Learning
    - How am I using my time before, during, and after class to master the information I need to learn? What area(s) do I need to focus my time working on? What can I do outside of school to prepare for the next day?
        - The student should create a schedule that includes "academic time" outside of school. This time may be used to check grades, complete missing assignments and homework, study, and/or organize materials. This may also include preparing materials, packing a book bag, making lunch, and picking out clothes for the next day. This will help the student to be on time for school without added stress due to rushing in the morning.
        - Utilize Time Wisely — Learning Form

---

**R.E.S.U.L.T.S.**
**Utilize Time Wisely – Learning**

Name _____     Date_____

How am I using my time before, during, and after school to practice the information I need to learn?

What area(s) do I need to focus my time working on?

What can I do outside of school to prepare for the next day?

| Reviewed with | Next steps |
|---|---|
|   |   |

- ○ Modified Planner
    - Calendars for long-term planning
    - Weekly planner pages with a section for each class
    - Time management section for planning after-school schedule
    - Goal section
    - Calendar Form
    - Weekly Planner Pages
    - Daily After-School Planning Pages
    - Goal Setting Pages
    - Alternative Learning and Personal Goal Setting Pages

R.E.S.U.L.T.S.

## R.E.S.U.L.T.S. Long-Term Assignment Tracking Form

Month_____ Year_____

| Monday | Tuesday | Wednesday | Thursday | Friday | Saturday | Sunday |
|--------|---------|-----------|----------|--------|----------|--------|
|        |         |           |          |        |          |        |
|        |         |           |          |        |          |        |
|        |         |           |          |        |          |        |
|        |         |           |          |        |          |        |
|        |         |           |          |        |          |        |
|        |         |           |          |        |          |        |

**Notes**

## R.E.S.U.L.T.S. Weekly Planner Pages

|  | Monday | Tuesday | Wednesday | Thursday | Friday | Saturday | Sunday |
|---|---|---|---|---|---|---|---|
| Before School | | | | | | | |
| Period ____ /Time ____ | | | | | | | |
| Period ____ /Time ____ | | | | | | | |
| Period ____ /Time ____ | | | | | | | |
| Period ____ /Time ____ | | | | | | | |
| Period ____ /Time ____ | | | | | | | |
| Period ____ /Time ____ | | | | | | | |
| Period ____ /Time ____ | | | | | | | |
| After School | | | | | | | |

R.E.S.U.L.T.S.

## R.E.S.U.L.T.S. After School Daily Schedule

Date _____

| Time | Activity/Assignment |
|---|---|
| 3:00 p.m. | |
| 3:30 p.m. | |
| 4:00 p.m. | |
| 4:30 p.m. | |
| 5:00 p.m. | |
| 5:30 p.m. | |
| 6:00 p.m. | |
| 6:30 p.m. | |
| 7:00 p.m. | |
| 7:30 p.m. | |
| 8:00 p.m. | |
| 8:30 p.m. | |
| 9:00 p.m. | |
| 9:30 p.m. | |

Be sure to pack up your bag, pack lunch, and pick out your clothes for the next day.

## R.E.S.U.L.T.S. Set Goals – Learning

Name _____          Date_____

My Current Grades:

| Subject | Teacher | Grade |
|---------|---------|-------|
|         |         |       |
|         |         |       |
|         |         |       |

My personal learning goal:

Three things I am going to do to achieve this goal:

Ways I can get help:

My support system:

R.E.S.U.L.T.S.

## R.E.S.U.L.T.S. Learning and Choices and Actions Goals

Week of _____

Learning Goal _____

Choices and Actions Goal _____

Document what you did each day to work toward your goals.

| Monday | Academic Goal |
|---|---|
| Date | Personal Goal |
| Tuesday | Academic Goal |
| Date | Personal Goal |
| Wednesday | Academic Goal |
| Date | Personal Goal |
| Thursday | Academic Goal |
| Date | Personal Goal |
| Friday | Academic Goal |
| Date | Personal Goal |

> **R.E.S.U.L.T.S.**
> **Promoting Positive Behavior and Responsibility for Learning**
>
> R - Review your current situation
> E - Evaluate your progress
> S - Self-assess
> U - Utilize time wisely
> **L - Lose the clutter**
> T - Take initiative
> S - Set goals

### L – Lose the Clutter

- Choices and Actions
    - What is holding me back from or standing in my way of being successful behaviorally? What steps do I need to take to overcome or eliminate my roadblock(s)?
        - The student should determine what things and which relationships may be standing in the way of success. The student should think about ways to eliminate the roadblock(s) holding him or her back from meeting with success. The student may need support in recognizing that some current activities and relationships may not be healthy or positive.
        - Lose the Clutter — Choices and Actions Form

**R.E.S.U.L.T.S.**
**Lose the Clutter – Choices and Actions**

Name _____     Date _____

What is holding me back or standing in my way from being successful behaviorally?

What steps do I need to take to overcome or eliminate the roadblocks that are holding me back?

| Reviewed with | Next steps |
|---|---|
|  |  |

- Learning
    - What is holding me back from or standing in my way of being successful academically? What steps do I need to take to overcome or eliminate my roadblock(s)?
        - The student should identify what is holding him or her back from being successful academically. The student should be taught effective time management, organizational, and study skills.
        - Lose the Clutter — Learning Form

---

**R.E.S.U.L.T.S.**
**Lose the Clutter – Learning**

Name _____          Date_____

What is holding me back or standing in my way of learning?




What steps do I need to take to overcome or eliminate the roadblocks that are holding me back?

---

| Reviewed with | Next steps |
|---|---|
|  |  |

> **R.E.S.U.L.T.S.**
> **Promoting Positive Behavior and Responsibility for Learning**
>
> R - Review your current situation
> E - Evaluate your progress
> S - Self-assess
> U - Utilize time wisely
> L - Lose the clutter
> **T - Take initiative**
> S - Set goals

### T – Take Initiative

- Choices and Actions
    - Whom can I go to for help? What should I say to ask for help?
        - The student should identify an adult whom he or she feels comfortable talking to and could approach when in need of help with issues. The student may need to be taught what to say to ask for help.
        - Take Initiative — Choices and Actions Form

## R.E.S.U.L.T.S.
## Take Initiative – Choices and Actions

Name _____     Date_____

List the name of an adult in our school whom you feel you could ask for help when you are struggling with a social or emotional issue. Why do you feel this is someone you can approach for help?

What can you say to ask for help with a social or emotional issue?

**R.E.S.U.L.T.S.**

- Learning
  - Whom can I go to for help? What should I say to ask for help?
    - The student should identify an adult whom he or she feels comfortable talking to and could approach when in need of help with issues. The student may need to be taught what to say to ask for help.
    - Take Initiative — Learning Form

---

**R.E.S.U.L.T.S.**
**Take Initiative – Learning**

Name _____        Date_____

List the name of an adult in our school whom you feel you could ask for help when you are struggling with learning. Why do you feel this is someone you can approach for help?




What can you say to ask for help with your learning?

---

> **R.E.S.U.L.T.S.**
> **Promoting Positive Behavior and Responsibility for Learning**
>
> R - Review your current situation
> E - Evaluate your progress
> S - Self-assess
> U - Utilize time wisely
> L - Lose the clutter
> T - Take initiative
> **S - Set goals**

### S – Set Goals

- Choices and Actions
    - What do I want to accomplish behaviorally during the next _____? (Choose a time frame that makes sense for the individual student: week, month, quarter, or semester.) What do I need to do to achieve this goal?
        - After processing the other steps in the R.E.S.U.L.T.S. framework, the student should identify what he or she wants to accomplish behaviorally over an agreed-upon time frame. The student should state his or her goal and the steps needed to accomplish this goal, including supports available to him or her. The student should document the steps he or she takes toward the goal in order to track progress.
        - Set Goals — Choices and Actions Form
        - Set Goals — Academic and Personal Goal Setting Form

## R.E.S.U.L.T.S.
### Set Goals – Choices and Actions

Name _____        Date_____

Describe something in your life you would like to change, improve upon, or do better:




My personal goal:




Three things I am going to do to achieve this goal:




Ways I can get help:




My support system:

- Learning
  - What do I want to accomplish academically during the next _____? (Choose a time frame that makes sense for the individual student: week, month, quarter, or semester.) What do I need to do to achieve this goal?
    - After processing the other steps in the R.E.S.U.L.T.S. framework, the student should identify what he or she wants to accomplish academically over an agreed-upon time frame. The student should state his or her goal and the steps needed to accomplish this goal, including supports available to him or her. The student should document the steps he or she takes toward the goal in order to track progress.
    - Set Goals — Learning Form
    - Set Goals — Academic and Personal Goal Setting Form

# R.E.S.U.L.T.S.

## R.E.S.U.L.T.S.
### Set Goals – Learning

Name _____     Date_____

My Current Grades:

| Subject | Teacher | Grade |
|---------|---------|-------|
|         |         |       |
|         |         |       |
|         |         |       |
|         |         |       |
|         |         |       |

My personal goal:


Three things I am going to do to achieve this goal:


Ways I can get help:


My support system:

## R.E.S.U.L.T.S. Choices and Actions/Learning Goals

Week of _____
Learning Goal _____
Choices and Actions Goal _____
Document what you did each day to work toward your goals.

| Monday | Academic Goal |
|---|---|
| Date | Personal Goal |
| Tuesday | Academic Goal |
| Date | Personal Goal |
| Wednesday | Academic Goal |
| Date | Personal Goal |
| Thursday | Academic Goal |
| Date | Personal Goal |
| Friday | Academic Goal |
| Date | Personal Goal |

**CHAPTER THREE**

# Recognizing the Function of Student Behavior: The Underlying Causes

**JON**

We all are bound to have good days and bad days. It is human nature to be affected by the experiences in our lives both big and small. All of us arrive at school with the best intentions of being positive, pleasant, and ready to facilitate stellar lessons, but it does not always translate to the product we put out. And let's keep in mind that we are the adults. So, when we consider student behavior, is it fair to always have a reactionary approach? Personally, I think of the conversations I have had with teachers asking why they reacted a certain way to a student, or why they struggled to teach to the best of their ability that day. Teachers tell me, "I was having a bad day" or, "I thought it was going to go better" or, "I just did not expect the student to do that." This is an error on us as adults because we are not preparing ourselves for what kids give us, their actions and reactions to everything they are thinking and feeling.

Behavior is a function of basic needs. You can cite your own saying here, but I like to think of it as the simplest of questions: "What do you need?" We ask it all the time when a student is in crisis, or even when a student just seems puzzled. Without that one small question and the opportunity for students to explain what they are feeling, we are making two mistakes. One, we are not equipping ourselves with all the information necessary to best serve that student. Two, we are robbing that student of the opportunity to learn how to effectively communicate what he or she needs to be successful. There is no perfect science to this. Students could be shut down before they arrive to your room. A student may refuse to share anything with you.

There are many strategies to break through to misunderstood students and understand the function of their behavior. You, the expert educator, most likely have a plethora of go-to strategies that work great for you. We would like to highlight two. First, control conversation by taking advantage of every opportunity to have a positive interaction with a student. Second, bring the conversation to the student's level; keep throwing out topics until something sticks. Once you have your topic, become an expert and make sure the kid knows it. It helps to use some informal language (appropriate, of course) that students use in their daily jargon.

Let's focus on the actual function of behavior. The first thing I typically do is investigate what happened immediately before the problem behavior took place. However, what we really need to determine is what is taking place outside of the classroom. This comes back to the importance of knowing all of your students and having a personal relationship built on trust.

Krista and I like to consider the peacock student. This is that child who needs time on stage at the start of the class, to feel like he is putting on a show to an extent. Oftentimes, we dread this student because these behaviors get in the way of what we, the adult, want to do. This is backward thinking that needs to be turned into a positive. Krista and I have a favorite student of ours who filled this classroom position perfectly. We encouraged teachers to use some basic strategies to counteract his need: meet him at the door, make seating during your opening flexible, keep the early part of class student-centered and interactive, etc. Most importantly, we encouraged a consistent, daily review of the expectations of those student-centered activities to empower the student to perform while controlling the outcome. However, we were missing the point.

Thankfully, a truly gifted teacher opened our eyes to the root function of his behavior. This student was the oldest of five kids, spread over twelve years.

Both parents worked swing shifts, meaning this 8th grader had to take the role of caretaker on a number of occasions. His younger siblings worshipped him, clinging to his every word, and he truly loved taking care of all of them. But he was fourteen years old and could not remember the last time his parents had time to give him any attention. The norm for this student was performing for his siblings, which made him feel valued and helped with the void he felt for attention. When the student came to school, he did not know how to gain attention on positive terms because he did not have any practice in it. This one gifted teacher asked the student about his family and allowed the student to share the whole story. Then, the teacher kept asking every day until he could finally tell the student, "Hey, that is great. Now I want to talk about *you*." The teacher made at least a few minutes a day sacred to talk about just the student. The student got to class early to have that time, or the teacher held him after or caught him before lunch. In a short amount of time, the teacher realized the student was insightful and opinionated—he just never had the chance, and therefore the skill, to interact that way appropriately. The student became a leader and the dividends paid off greatly in other classes.

I tell you that story to share a success, but more importantly to highlight our best strategy. Knowing the student well made the teacher able to tell when the student maybe did not get sleep or was stressed. The teacher knew when to create an opportunity for the student to share his feelings. This is the key to recognizing the function of behavior.

Krista and I always look at behavior as filling three basic needs.

## Function 1
### The student wants to avoid something.

Students may know they are unprepared for an assessment, or know they did not understand an assignment, so they are not interested in participating. This is common; they are kids. How often do we as adults convince ourselves to push off things we do not want to do, making every excuse in the world to not do it? We do a pretty good job justifying our lack of action. It is not just about schoolwork: students can avoid working with specific peers or interacting with adults. There is plenty to avoid in the course of a school day.

**Strategy 1:** To get ahead of this problem, teach the skills that support the content. If you know a student struggles to study, sacrifice instructional time or utilize intervention time to teach study skills and grow the ability to review information. If a student does not work well independently or outside of school, provide choice. Give students options of when to complete the work, or allow students to demonstrate their learning in different ways. In the worst-case scenario, when you can't get ahead of the problem, go back to the most important question you can ever ask a student: "What do you need?" This is not a theory; this is a practice. "What do you need from me? How can I help?"

Krista and I are big believers in the word *yet*. A student does not work independently yet, or does not know how to study yet. So, choose the option of showing students you are here to help.

## Function 2
### The student wants to gain a preferred activity.

This is different from avoiding a task. A student is expected to do an opening activity, but is chomping at the bit to work on a project. Rather than following the expectations, the student tries to speed up the bellringer, or opening activity, by asking the teacher to cut down the time, or yelling at a classmate to stop talking so the class can move on. This is disruptive, so naturally you address it.

**Strategy 2:** This behavior may be perceived as rude or disrespectful and is addressed as such. Unfortunately, the student had no intention of being rude or disrespectful, and the outburst was countered by telling the student how it was perceived in front of peers. The behavior can't be ignored, so often a power struggle ensues. Take this strategy as a two-part approach. First, use your knowledge of the student as a person to ask a leading question: "Hey, help me out. What's up? What are you trying to do right now?" Hear that student out; he or she may tell you flat out about wanting to work on the project, or the student may become annoyed. The latter shouldn't bother you because you are gaining valuable information and the opportunity to remind the student you are there for him or her. Secondly, prep your activities really well. When I was teaching, I knew when kids were looking at a deadline or were looking forward to an activity. As part of opening my class, I explained, "I know we are really excited to get moving on our newspaper articles, but we have to get with the program. We always start our day together by activating." Then, I reviewed the expectations, asked for questions, concerns, and comments, and we hit the ground running. I gave up thirty seconds of time to avoid a situation that could cost me 3–5 minutes on a good day. On a bad day, I would lose the whole period.

## Function 3
## The student is seeking attention.

The student wants to be noticed. The student not only wants to be noticed, but wants to be noticed immediately. Even more difficult, he or she is not concerned in the least about the terms of being recognized. This is the scariest of functions, in my opinion, because it seems unpredictable what words or actions can make the situation worse. We all experience that need for attention that ultimately clouds the basic need of acceptance.

*Strategy 3:* I go back to that basic need of acceptance. Each student wants to feel he or she belongs to something. At the middle level especially, students may not know what they want to belong to. This gives us the precious opportunity to steer students toward a positive sense of belonging. That is how we should manage our class.

Flood the class with positive feedback for the group that has attention-seeking students. Tell them you like their shoes in front of the whole class, loudly. Then, tell them quietly you really appreciate them sitting down or helping you get started. Be a dictator of positivity, making it a mandate that everyone feels the love.

Talk to your colleagues about kids. Find out what is going on out there as the students move through the trenches. This step will equip you with knowing what to talk about. A favorite of mine, when I know a student is not getting along with a peer or another teacher, is to show my human side. I will tell the kid, "You know what, I don't always get along with some of the people I work with. Even worse, this kid in my first period is driving me nuts. On top of that, my dog pooped on the carpet this morning." Hey, I gave the student attention, and hopefully an out to vent what is bothering him or her.

## *Provide opportunity and take chances.*

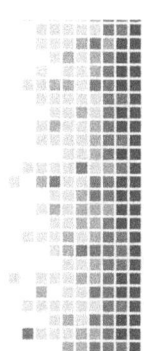

Provide opportunity and take chances. Consider that sentence in every structure you put in place. When grouping students, put the attention-seeking student with a preferred peer and make the sacrifice of some off-task behavior to avoid a power struggle. Try new activities that raise engagement, allowing yourself to facilitate rather than deliver. If it goes bad for a day, take it as a learning opportunity and try something new.

If we want to understand underlying causes of behavior, knowing our kids will always be our best tool. I will tell you honestly that most strategies we offer do involve sacrificing some instructional time. All the strategies run parallel to teaching and reteaching your expectations explicitly. Equip yourself with the most knowledge possible about the individual student; it keeps you ahead of the curve. Creativity goes a long way when structuring your class. In the moment, when things are going bad, hold on to the philosophy that we are there to serve them, not the other way around. Then ask the question, "What do you need?"

# CHAPTER FOUR
# Connections

### KRISTA

Jon and I cannot think of any other way to start this chapter than to strongly recommend that you put this book down and do an internet search for Rita Pierson's TED talk "Every Kid Needs a Champion."[1] Do it. We are serious . . . but please come back after you watch it!

Welcome back! Wow, right? We are not sure if there is anything left to say after that, but we will try! We have shared this video many, many times over the past few years. We share it at the first back-to-school faculty meeting, during that long stretch between winter break and spring break, as a send-off at the end of the year, during new teacher induction, and at orientation meetings for every student teacher who comes into the building.

In seven minutes and forty-eight seconds, Pierson sums up the epitome of the importance of making connections with students. At the time this chapter was written, her TED talk had been viewed 8,496,028 times! Just imagine if every one of the educators who watched the video made a deep and lasting connection with their students! The results would be astounding and life changing.

---

[1] Pierson, Rita. "Every Kid Needs a Champion." https://www.ted.com/talks/rita_pierson_every_kid_needs_a_champion?language=en

The responsibility of being an educator goes well beyond teaching curriculum, monitoring progress, assigning projects, testing, and grading. Pierson said, "Every child deserves a champion: an adult who will never give up on them, who understands the power of connection and insists they become the best they can possibly be." It is a tall order to be "that adult," but if we choose to take on the title "educator," we owe it to our students to take that role seriously.

Not all of our students come to us with a strong support system. We are the support system and place of safety for some of them. They may not show it in the kindest and most positive ways all of the time, but we are some of our kids' best hopes of being successful and happy in life. Let that sink in.

The summer after my first year as assistant principal, I was in my office working and heard a student who was talking with our secretary. I yelled, "Hey, Ethan! Come back and say hello to me!"

He walked back to my office with a surprised look on his face. I asked him what was wrong, and he said, "I can't believe you recognized me by my voice." I will never forget the big smile that flashed across his face when I told him that I'd know him and his voice anywhere. That right there is a connection!

There are some kids we would have taken home with us if we could. We held sobbing children in our arms after they disclosed something that was weighing heavily on their hearts and minds, we visited students at their homes, and we walked with kids and reassured them that they were strong and capable of making changes in their lives as they were placed into police cars. Some connections run deep and feel like they take all you have, but not all connections have to be grand in nature all the time.

Small connections, little interactions between you and your students, are all that are needed to begin a relationship that could last well beyond the school year that you have together. These connections can make all the difference—like the elementary teacher who is invited year after year as an honored guest to graduation long after he taught these students. What higher honor is there as an educator than to be remembered because you made a difference in your students' lives?

# R.E.S.U.L.T.S.

*Small connections, little interactions between you and your students, are all that is needed to begin a relationship that could last well beyond the school year that you have together and can make all the difference –*

Kids need to know that you care, that you notice things they say and do, that you recognize that they are unique, and that they are important to you. We know that this is easier said than done with some students. Some make it very difficult for others to love them, but overwhelmingly they are usually the ones who want and need it the most.

I often think about a student whom many would have characterized as a punk. There were probably teachers who did a silent happy dance on days he was absent. He was impulsive, sometimes rude, and a lot of times said things that thoroughly made his teachers see red. We had countless conversations with him about choices, and how frustrating it was for people when they did things to try to help him and he treated them disrespectfully in return. He almost always felt remorse after the fact, and he wanted to make good choices, but he really struggled to figure it out in the moment.

He loved us one day and cursed us out the next. But do you know what? To this day, years later, he keeps coming back. He seeks us out, emails, calls, and stops in when he needs help or to tell us something exciting in his life. Why? Because he knows we love him; we stuck by him and will never give up on him—*no matter what!*

Forging relationships with kids does not have to start on day one, but it is a perfect time to start. Actually, before day one is even better. If you have your class list during the summer, send a letter home or email your students to introduce yourself. Tell them what they can expect for your class and a little bit about yourself. Invite the students to reply with their hopes and fears for the upcoming year and anything they wish to share about themselves with you. This creates a window into their world and demonstrates to your students and their families that you are interested and approachable.

I cannot stress enough how important it is for teachers and administrators to be present as students arrive at school. We know it is prime time to hold meetings, but we get only one chance to start the day off right. Be available to welcome each child to school and say good morning. If every staff member is out and about saying hello to the children, there is a good chance that each student could be addressed multiple times in a positive way before classes even begin! This is powerful and creates a "soft landing" for them that communicates they are safe and welcome and that we are excited to see them.

I ask my teachers to treat our students the way they want others in their positions to treat their own children, or children for whom they care deeply. This is different than treating students the way we treat our own children, because there is a difference between how we raise our own children, as parents, and how we would want others to interact with our children. When I am interacting with a student, I always think to myself, *I hope this is how my son's principal would treat him if he were in this situation.* My expectation is that he would be listened to, shown respect and compassion, held accountable if necessary, and given the opportunity to reflect and make changes.

Most children thrive on the love and attention they receive from their families, friends, and school community. Some struggle because they are lacking in an area or two, and some still struggle even with attention and care from everyone in their lives. These situations require us to be creative and continue to search for and try different strategies until something works—for the long haul.

We had two girls who were relentless toward each other. There were screaming matches in the halls and physical fights in and outside of school, and the families of both girls were even feuding with each other over their daughters' situation. We assigned disciplinary consequences, had meetings with the girls individually and together, brought parents in to meet with us, and the local police even got involved. Nothing seemed to work. If one of them looked in the other's direction, it caused an uproar. I think the fact that they were breathing the same air even annoyed them!

We could have continued to pile on the discipline and spend more of our time addressing the same issues over and over. But we were thoroughly convinced that if things kept going down this road it was only going to end badly for everyone.

I decided that I had to act outside of the traditional way we would normally handle situations like this. I met with each of the girls individually and asked her what her favorite food was from one of our local Italian restaurants. Then I invited them to lunch with me. I told them that I did not care if they spoke to each other or even looked at each other, but that the three of us were going to sit at the same table and eat lunch together. I ordered wings, French fries, pizza, and salad and put the food out on the table with cute paper plates and napkins.

I have to be honest here. I was nervous and was praying that a food fight would not erupt, but in the end, there were smiles, giggles, stories shared, and even a photo of the two of them with their arms around each other. The girls found out that most of what they were upset about was misinformation given to them by others who were clearly trying to stir the pot and cause trouble. We had a good conversation about how people claiming to be our friends would never put us in a situation like that—an unfortunate life lesson learned.

One of the highlights of my year was calling both mothers and telling them how proud I was of the girls for how mature and kind they were during our lunch. That day ended the drama between those two. I am hopeful that the girls will take this experience of trusting me and showing compassion and forgiveness toward each other with them and apply it in other situations that come up in their lives. Did it take some extra effort, time, and money? Yes, but trust me—it was so worth it!

Teaching the curriculum and ensuring that you are able to accomplish all of your objectives for the class period is essential, but so is creating relationships and making connections. Setting aside a short amount of time at the start of the class period for students to share, open up, and express themselves with the teacher and peers creates a sense of community. It is a time when interpersonal needs are met, which may set students up to be more focused on the lesson since they were given the opportunity to share what was on their minds.

We know that your time is precious and that you have contracted hours that you are required to be at work, but being available to students throughout the day at times other than class time goes a long way. Opening up in front of a crowd or during class is not very comfortable for some students.

Have you ever shown up at a kid's soccer game, or even a non-school-sponsored event like a ballet recital? It blows their minds! Just imagine if you were the only person who showed up for them. That is powerful . . . and sad, but it is the reality. We always have to remember that we may be "it" for some of our kids.

We were introduced to the Two by Ten strategy by a dear friend and colleague with whom we have spent many hours over the course of a year, working with students with significant challenging behaviors. The premise of the Two by Ten strategy is that the teacher chooses the most challenging student and spends two minutes a day for ten consecutive days talking to that student about anything appropriate that interests the student. In a study,[2] psychologist Raymond Wlodkowski states that research shows teachers who use the Two by Ten strategy find an 85 percent improvement in that child's behavior. The study also suggests that the behavior of the whole class improves as well!

What kind of crazy magic strategy is this? Have you ever heard of anything in education that has this kind of return? Eighty-five percent improvement? Wow! We'd say it is definitely worth a shot. Obviously, it comes down to the student feeling valued, heard, seen, and cared for. The effort and compassion on the part of the educator is the real magic!

To bring this chapter full circle, we'll end with another powerful Rita Pierson quote: "We can do this. We're educators. We're born to make a difference."

---

[2] https://www.teachhub.com/two-ten-classroom-management-method.

## CHAPTER FIVE
# Is What's Good for Us Good for Our Students?

### KRISTA

We are going to get real and be pretty frank in discussing this next topic. It might get a little bit uncomfortable, but we feel that we can "go there" because most educators, the two of us included, have in some shape or form been guilty of engaging in this behavior. Let's face it head on, together.

So, please read this chapter with an open mind and take some time to reflect. If you determine that you do some of these things, please consider changes you could make to ensure you are being fair and reasonable while holding students to high standards. If you never engage in these types of behaviors, you are a rock star and we are in awe of you. Please keep it up! Shout it from the rooftops and continue to be a role model for others.

We believe that students should be held to high standards and expectations as well as treated reasonably and with compassion. The most important fact to keep in mind during this discussion is that there is a difference between an adult—who has an extensive education, degrees, life experience, and a level of maturity—and a student who is still learning concepts, time management, and organization skills while experiencing all kinds of biological changes!

As working adults, we have supervisors, deadlines, and expectations that we are to meet, but have you ever done any of the following things: turn your lesson plans in late, call out sick because you want to avoid something, grade papers or check email during a professional development session, volunteer for an after-school event and then not attend, slip out of a faculty meeting to get a drink, use the restroom, or stretch your legs, or take a personal day when you need a day for your own mental health? We are willing to bet most of us can say yes to at least one of these types of behaviors that we, as adults, choose to do to meet our own needs and schedules.

Kids typically do not have these options available to them, and the consequences for these types of behaviors are normally not very pleasant. A student who turns work in late usually loses points or gets a zero, may receive a phone call home, and possibly loses privileges. If a student walks out of class because he or she is bored, not seeing the value in the lesson, or is frustrated or tired of listening to the teacher, that student would be written up. If a student works on an assignment for another subject during class, the assignment would probably be taken away in front of the whole class, all of the work lost, and possibly graded as a zero. If a student texts on a cell phone, this may result in the confiscation of the cell phone, a phone call home, and some type of behavioral consequence.

Just think of the outrage if we, as adults, were treated the same way for doing these types of things. Would your principal withhold your paycheck because you did not meet a deadline? Would you be told that you could not participate in a dress-down day because you were two minutes late for school? Would a supervisor take the papers you are grading from you in front of the rest of the faculty during a PD session? Now, some of these behaviors are just plain rude and unprofessional and should be avoided at all costs. Hopefully a supervisor would bring this to your attention in a supportive but direct way. But we simply wouldn't tolerate some of the consequences that we inflict on students for the very same behaviors.

It's important to recognize that we, as adults, are allotted some leeway, second chances, and opportunities to make adjustments to our lives and schedules that our students usually aren't afforded. Please understand that we do not think it is okay to let students slide on everything and get away with things they should be held accountable for, but we need to show compassion and understanding and teach students how to respectfully and responsibly advocate for themselves to meet their needs when things come up.

That is how life works: we can try, but we do not work at 100 percent all of the time. We are human, and things come up in our lives. Sometimes we need to create or request allowances so that we may reset ourselves and then get back at it. It is important to consider that our kids go through similar experiences but don't always have the freedom we do, as adults, to create the opportunities they need to get through whatever they are experiencing.

We cannot tell you how many times we have heard people say that they take points off of a late assignment or give kids zeros because "we need to teach responsibility." Having a conversation with a student and teaching how to appropriately manage time for the next assignment, how to study for the next test, how to ask for help, what to do when family or personal issues come up, and what strategies he or she can use when bored will go a lot further in "teaching responsibility" than penalizing students through their grades or a behavioral consequence.

We go back to this point a million times: strong relationships with students are the first line of defense for most situations. If you have a connection with your students and create a classroom/school culture of trust and support, having tough conversations with students is a lot easier. Also, if students trust you and know you are on their side, they are more apt to take to heart what you are saying to them.

> ... *strong relationships with students are the first line of defense for most situations.*

Some students struggle with asking for help because they (1) do not realize they need it, and (2) don't know what to say to ask for help. When a positive relationship exists, you can say, "Hey, bud. I have noticed you are struggling. I think you might need some help." Imagine the weight that could be lifted off of a student's shoulders just by hearing those words from someone he trusts and knows genuinely wants to help.

Even when students recognize they need help, sometimes they do not know how to ask. Maybe they have tried in the past and did not receive the support they required. Maybe they are too shy or too proud to speak up. Whatever the reason, while they are practicing this skill, just give them the words.

This is an example of a form we use at midpoint when checking grades. All students who have earned a 70 percent or less in at least one class receive this form and are expected to take it to each of their teachers to review and discuss what they are able to do to improve their grade(s). Also, on the back is a script that students can use when approaching their teachers. This helps give courage to students by providing them with the words they may not have.

### Academic Check-In Day Form

Dear _____,

As of _____, you have earned a 70% or below in my class. I am contacting you to make sure that you are aware of this and to encourage you to take steps to make improvements. **The 3rd Quarter ends on Monday, March 27th.**

| Course | Grade | Teacher |
|--------|-------|---------|
|        |       |         |

When we meet, we will discuss the following steps you may take to improve your grade and to learn the important information for this class:

## R.E.S.U.L.T.S.

- 
- 
- 

Be sure to take home all materials you will need in order to perform the steps we have discussed. Please share this information with your parents. If you need any assistance or have any questions, let me know.

You can do it! I believe in you and am here to help.
Thank you,
—*(Signature)*

### Tips to help you take responsibility for your learning

- Set aside "academic time" each evening. You can use this time to complete homework but you should set aside time even if you don't have homework. You may want to organize your materials, check your grades, check the assignments posted on our website, update your planner, review your notes from the day, read your book for ELA, or read/reread in Science or Social Studies.
- Pick out your clothes and pack your lunch, backpack and gym bag the night before. Make sure you have everything ready to go before you go to bed so that you don't forget anything you may need and you have enough time in the morning to get ready without being rushed.
- Ask for help when you need it.

### Don't know what to say to ask for help? Try this!

Mr./Mrs. _____ I would like to be more successful in your class. Could you please help me figure out what I can do? What ideas do you have to help me stay up-to-date on my assignments and prepare for assessments?

## CHAPTER SIX
# Explicitly Teaching Skills

**KRISTA**

Students do not wake up in the morning and think to themselves, *How can I make my teacher's life miserable and screw up in front of my peers today?* Behaviors have stories behind them—stories that can't be fixed by throwing discipline at them. Everyone wants to be successful. Everyone wants to feel included and accepted. When students do not know the expectations and have not met with enough success following the expectations—along with a plethora of other factors such as trauma, issues that come along with poverty, biological imbalances (the list can go on and on)—the fact still remains that kids want to be successful, be accepted, and fit in.

*Behaviors have stories behind them- stories that can't be fixed by throwing discipline at them.*

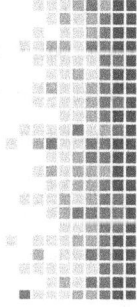

## R.E.S.U.L.T.S.

We have a responsibility to explicitly teach students expectations, coping and resiliency skills, and how to ask for help so that they may navigate the times when they do not feel in control or they are in crisis mode.

When we present about explicitly teaching skills, we use two videos we found on the web. They both feature an eleven- or twelve-year-old child's first encounter with a rotary phone. The first video[1] involves a girl and her grandmother. The grandmother is appalled that the girl does not know how the phone works. She keeps saying, "It's a phone! You dial it! What do you mean you don't know how?" She acts upset with her granddaughter, who truly does not seem to know how to use the phone. Although the girl tries a few methods, her grandmother continues to criticize her for not knowing how to use it, and repeats, "It's a phone! What's wrong with you?"

In the second video[2] there is a boy and a man who is probably the boy's dad. They are visiting the boy's great-grandfather. The boy is intrigued by the rotary phone and asks how it works. There is some teasing, but then the father tells the boy to pick up the receiver and listen for a dial tone, explains what a dial tone is, and then tells him to dial the first number. When the boy struggles with this task, the dad says, "Put your finger in the hole and push the dial over to the silver thing and then let go." The boy then finishes dialing his number. When asked if it worked, he pulls his smartphone out of his pocket with a huge smile on his face and holds it up, showing that it is ringing.

The first video reminds me of when students act out and we tell them they need to behave, focus, or stop. Some students do not know what that means or how to do it. Maybe they have not ever really been taught. Maybe they have not had enough practice, or maybe they haven't met with success enough times to learn that it feels a lot better to follow the expectation than to constantly get in trouble.

If the grandmother took a few minutes to show her granddaughter how to

---

1 "Teenager Doesn't Know How to Use Rotary Phone" via YouTube user RM Videos. https://www.youtube.com/watch?v=iIoVkWGm8ec.

2 "The 2016 Rotary Phone Challenge" via YouTube user Patti Masa. https://www.youtube.com/watch?v=EO5R_pFdRFU.

dial the phone, I'm betting she could have successfully made the call. Instead, unhelpful information was said over and over. In the scenario with the boy, his father taught him step by step what to do, and in less than ninety seconds he successfully made a call.

If we take time to explicitly teach what it is that we want students to do or not do, we will have more success, and so will they!

# CHAPTER SEVEN
# Consequences vs. Learning Opportunities

## JON

The traditional system in place at most schools dictates that we wait around for students to make mistakes. After a first mistake is made, a teacher or counselor or administrator has a conversation with the student about the incident. Most of the questions are related to trying to get the student to recognize the mistake and take some accountability for it. School counselors want to keep their conversations about choices and keep their input supportive, encouraging the student to do better (I base this off my own experiences with the fantastic counselors I have worked with). The conversation with the teacher or administrator will almost certainly end with a negative consequence no matter how positive the conversation may have gone. This is a trend we have tried to curb in our experience together. If a student disrupts class one time, to the point we have to be involved, we feel he or she deserves a chance to restore that situation. There have been a number of students to whom, thankfully, we were able to explain where they went wrong, and how to rectify the situation. This is great—a victory, a beacon of light in an otherwise ugly business. However, it is not the consistent reality we exist in. More typically, the reason we are speaking with the student stems from a number of factors that brought us to the point where we feel obligated to provide a consequence. For the 5–7 percent of students who require the most intervention, the consequence will begin the attritional process of stacking discipline and increasing the severity of consequences.

There is merit to this process. A student makes a mistake, and we attach discipline to accountability to serve as a deterrent against any negative behaviors in the future. The severe or frequent incident constitutes graver consequences, hoping to be an even bigger reminder that the negative behavior is unacceptable. This is all very boring and common sense, but it has been my life for three years as we have tried to change this approach. The issue is that it is always reactionary. Every educator we speak with has the same theory in mind: let's be proactive. What can we do before things start happening? Awesome concept—I agree wholeheartedly. It is the very reason we have spent years forming a three-tiered intervention plan in addition to our other job duties. What we have to consider is that despite the best supports, students will still make mistakes and not respond to intervention. That is how the concept of learning opportunities came to life.

What is a consequence really? In the situation just described, a consequence is a reaction to a negative behavior. Usually, this involves the loss of a preferred activity for the student, or a restriction of the student's free time (lunch, after school, etc.). The student spends the time in mandatory silence or working on schoolwork. A student doing academic work while serving a consequence is hard to argue with, and he or she has to take advantage of any opportunity to be academically successful. However, in our experience, our traditional consequences were creating more work for us. Our in-school suspension plan was creating a lot of calls for administrative support. After-school detention tended to be a frustrated teacher trying to keep kids silent, or a complete mess of out-of-control students. There is an additional function of the handed-out discipline to discuss: support of the teachers. Yes, we will say it again—teachers need consequences. The faculty wants discipline to be handed out swiftly and consistently in order to feel supported. We truly believe every teacher wants to help a child grow and succeed. Therefore, we must respond with discipline when learning is disrupted, a teacher is disrespected, or property is damaged—and the list goes on. Instead of focusing on tradition, we chose to focus on part of the consequence: the time.

The pure similarity between traditional consequences and learning opportunities is the concept of time served. Truthfully, when using learning opportunities, students are still serving the consequence of time. We have simply chosen to flip the thinking of what a consequence accomplishes. Every mistake a student makes in your building is an opportunity to make a change. Using learning opportunities involves taking structured activities that are tailored to the individual student and the individual situation. Learning opportunities strive to provide meaningful structure to the time students serve.

> *Every mistake a student makes in your building is an opportunity to make a change.*

Learning opportunities rely on four strong components and benefits. We can view these benefits as a comparison to what traditional consequences provide or are unable to provide.

1. **Traditional consequences provide support to teachers by providing a timely response to a discipline incident.**

   Learning Opportunity: By using the consequence to provide a learning opportunity, teachers are supported even more. The time is used for students to process the incident through the use of R.E.S.U.L.T.S. Furthermore, students are using the time as an academic intervention with established steps. These actions provide a chance to decrease negative behavior.

2. **Traditional consequences serve as a deterrent against future negative behavior.**

<u>Learning Opportunity</u>: The concept of having a learning opportunity deters negative student behaviors in two ways. First, students may truly dislike going through steps or activities and want to avoid being subject to them again. This is great—if a student is able to change his or her behavior with little intervention, that is a bonus. Second, the added dynamic of the learning opportunity breaks the mold of, "You did wrong. Don't do wrong again." Now students have to interact with the idea of explaining why there was an issue.

3. **Traditional consequences are not typically collaborative or beneficial to all stakeholders.**

<u>Learning Opportunity</u>: As you expand your learning opportunities and have a handle on using R.E.S.U.L.T.S., more benefits become present. It may feel unlikely at first, but students will respond to the opportunity to talk about situations that are taking place. Rather than a student serving a consequence and being told, "Let's not let this happen again," we are creating partnerships within the learning opportunity. As the staff members, we can learn about the students and help our colleagues gain valuable insight into managing a particular student's behavior. Even more important, the learning opportunity is the perfect place for reviewing expectations and practice.

4. **Traditional consequences do not typically provide an opportunity for a positive relationship or restorative action.**

<u>Learning Opportunity</u>: I use the word *typically* very cautiously here. Many people have used reflection or letters of apology or some mode of providing meaningful opportunity for the student to reconcile the situation—all great practices, especially when teachers do it within their own assigned consequences that they manage. However, consistent practice has been difficult, at least for us. When you think of a learning opportunity, stay away from the

term *detention monitor*. Think more along the lines of *learning facilitator*. By using R.E.S.U.L.T.S., a student can gain a valuable relationship with an adult that can be expanded. The student can leave the consequence having learned or grown, and now that relationship can be on positive terms.

The learning opportunity additionally serves as a built-in process for re-teaching expectations. As we have said before, explicitly taught expectations are crucial for the universal success of your classroom, or even the whole building. If a student does not seem to understand the expectations, it is completely appropriate to believe that he or she has not learned the expectations yet or has not had enough practice. Learning opportunities focus on fixing that issue. A student can serve the consequence without getting better, if we allow. When our reaction to an incident is a learning opportunity, we provide students with a clearer understanding of what they are being asked to do and, if necessary, additional practice.

As long as we have schools, we will have discipline to deal with. We will continue to focus on intervention, providing students the support they need before academic or behavioral issues occur. However, to truly have the whole package, we need to have the right structure for responding to discipline incidents. What we are encouraging through learning opportunities, is getting rid of the knee-jerk reaction consequences. We have to accept that no matter what we do, whatever incident or mistake took place is not going away. Our duty then becomes providing an opportunity for that student to grow.

## CHAPTER EIGHT
# Make Detention and In-School Suspension Learning Opportunities

**JON**

de•ten•tion
[dē'ten(t)SH(e)n]
Noun

An online search of the definition of detention gave us this:
- The action of detaining someone or the state of being detained in official custody
- The punishment of being kept in school after hours

Sounds awful. Purely punishment. No learning, remediation, or improvement being made. It's something we do to demonstrate that a code of conduct or policy is being enforced, but as for effectiveness, does it really deter students or fix a problem behavior? We don't think so.

We have asked many students what value they find in detention, the act of being held after school or at lunch to miss their free time. Most students tell us it stinks, or they shrug their shoulders and do not offer much of an opinion. A better question we have asked is, "What do your teachers do when they have an issue with you in class?" This question brought on much more emotional responses. Many students told us about their parents being called, which caused trouble for them at home. To this news, we of course smiled. Teachers reaching out to parents is a very important step in creating success for a student. We have to keep preaching how important it is to harness parental support whenever possible. Also, we want to control that line of communication and keep parents informed always. There is one hang-up: the parent is not in school with the student, and most likely the consequence at home is only punitive, forced compliance for fear of lost time playing video games or using the cell phone. That means it is only a bandage, a temporary fix. Parents are great—they teach children how to be adults. We are looking at the following: What is our duty at the school to assist the parent? Teach kids subject matter, and help them grow as readers, writers, and learners? Yes, absolutely! Will that alone ever be enough? No, absolutely not.

So we know students dislike consequences, the loss of their time, or the boredom of isolation from their peers. However, despite consistent opportunities for after-school detention, lunch detention, in-school suspension, and teacher detentions, discipline did not decrease. This made it clear to us that we were throwing the same solutions at a growing problem and wondering why things did not get better.

Learning opportunity does not just refer to the students. We realized that we were missing opportunities for empowerment of our teachers. By developing structured strategies with materials guiding what teachers could do in restriction, we saw faculty take ownership of their own domains. More importantly, we saw more teachers taking advantage of their own learning opportunity, a chance to learn more about their kids. There was a cycle that needed to be broken: a student shows a negative behavior, and we react with negative language and a consequence. Far too many times the teacher was reacting to the behavior, but then not providing the consequence. When the teacher has the learning opportunity to discover the root cause of the behavior within the consequence outside of class, the student has a much better chance of feeling supported. Learning about the student and building a positive relationship is the most important aspect of supporting the student.

> *Learning about the student and building a positive relationship is the most important aspect of supporting the student.*

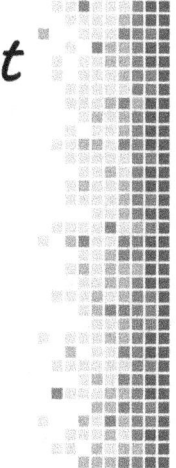

Teachers and administrators are all experts and have their own style for interacting with students. This is no different in providing intervention and behavior support. For the best practices of utilizing R.E.S.U.L.T.S. and creating a learning opportunity for students, we offer these basic steps.

### Involve Parents

Whether it is a teacher running a restriction, or the administrative response of a detention, we want parents to be informed. Calling to communicate the problem in the classroom, or the nature of some disruption, is a great logical step. When making a restriction into a learning opportunity, we want parents to know the purpose of the restriction, the action steps that are going to be taken, and the ultimate goal of that learning opportunity. This builds a relationship with the parents and helps them know that the actions of their students are being met with support from the school district.

## Have Students Identify What the Detention Is For

We can easily tell a student, "You are serving detention for (insert reason here)." Then we can give students a long list of expectations they must follow during their restriction with the threat hanging over their heads of additional consequences. We have seen students struggle to follow additional expectations when they have already not met the building expectations. Rather than dictating the reasons to students, make a discussion out of why they are facing a consequence. Use leading questions that generate conversations rather than just asking about the incident.

> "How do you feel about the way Mr. Treese talked to you during class?"
> "Can you explain to me how the cafeteria works? What is everyone expected to do?"
> "Who is this kid you are having a problem with? It sounds like a crappy deal."

The goal is to get students to explain in their own words what happened and why.

## Attach Academics

Consider the reality in which your typical student with behavior issues exists. In our building, students with difficult behaviors also have huge academic roadblocks hindering their success. They have been told they are not doing well, and quite possibly they have started acting out because they are incapable of handling what they perceive as negative feedback. Believe us when we say we know kids quite often have the wrong perception of their conversations with teachers. Even when a teacher is being over-the-moon supportive, students can still see it as a singling out. Therefore, when we consider attaching academics to a restriction, we do not mean to take another opportunity to tell students how their grades stink or dictate to them what they must do. *The only option is to make your interactions an offering of support.* Look at a student's grades, and then ask her what she does not like about specific classes. A personal practice of mine is telling students areas I struggled in, or dumb mistakes I made through my schooling. Attaching academics is about showing our human side while helping students to be able to communicate what holds them back.

- Review the grades and know where students stand.
- Ask the questions to help students identify their barriers or what they need to do.
- Be actionable. What is a tangible step students can take for their academics?

In addition, please note that we want to take any opportunity we have to provide academic support to students. If we have students restricted who want to work on academics, we make that happen.

### Do Not Require Silence—Facilitate the Noise

Students can learn very well by independently completing an activity and asking for the help of the teacher if necessary. Is this how we structure our classes the majority of the time? We are sure most of you said no. If we are spending the consequence of time, do we really need to spend the consequence of silence? We would say no, but we qualify that statement by encouraging you to facilitate the noise. If students are talking about an issue among peers, engage in it, figure out the root causes, and start offering advice. Students will not settle from talking about their music or sports figures, so jump in the conversation, ask questions, or play the music. As you are engaging in these conversations, strategize how to circle back to a school-related topic. This is the step where we are valuing relationship over progress. It pains us to know people will cringe at the thought of students accomplishing less by being noisy in a restricted consequence. To that we say, isn't the building of a relationship, the support of a student, the recognizing of a student viewpoint, progress also? Krista has a mantra about student success that has been shared with most professionals in our district. In essence, everybody just needs that one person to care, or that one conversation to encourage them from being unsuccessful to becoming a success story. It is that important. Many students sit on that wall and could fall either way. We would hate to see the need for silence cause a missed opportunity to support a student.

## Be Creative

I affectionately refer to this as the "continue the performance" step. Every teacher is performing all day every day. I once had a student teaching supervisor who told me that teaching was like getting on stage every day with the best plan in place, but no knowledge of who the hecklers will be—meaning that school is unpredictable, but with experience we get a better handle on how to work the crowd. Being creative allows you the opportunity to do that more effectively. Programming and materials are great. They build a process students go through and they help with consistency among staff members. Some materials should not be spelled out for professionals. Try different things, make kids move, or play board games with different rules. The students have already made mistakes, and nobody is asking you to create miracles, so what do you have to lose? In my years as dean of students, I have never made students' lives more difficult by making them share one thing they like about school to pass "Go," and one thing they hate about school to get out of jail. If you start a reflection activity and it is flat, or kids are resisting, scrap it, reset, and think to yourself, *If I had to do this, what would I need to be doing along with it to make it enjoyable?* Then, run with it. Using R.E.S.U.L.T.S. and creating learning opportunities is not a one-size-fits-all, overnight success story. Everyone needs to take a framework and make it their own.

## Always Reflect

There are many ways to consider what we have done in the past and learn from those experiences. The importance lies not in choosing the perfect reflection activity, but rather in creating the action of reflecting on whatever way works. Some students do really well answering questions and describing what happened and what they could have done differently. We want to push students to be able to communicate in this way because language skills will always be important. However, we can differentiate reflection just like we differentiate instruction. If reflection is considered an assessment of students' understanding of the situation they created, it can't be appropriate to dictate that students respond by writing an answer to the question. We should be creating opportunities for students to express themselves. What we concern ourselves with first and foremost is the student showing the ability to reflect. We will always find a way to reflect, but let students use reflection as a means of expression. This step is key: no matter how we make it happen, every student should reflect before leaving any restriction. This is the learning opportunity through which students learn about understanding themselves.

Also, as teachers, we can use student reflection to help us grow professionally. Krista and I feel that we have both grown as educators by learning from students.

## Build a Plan

We want to make our learning opportunities actionable. Building a plan is not necessarily a step-by-step process for success. The focus is more on making actionable items that the individual student is capable of doing. If a student would benefit from having a teacher sign a planner to make sure he or she knows the assignments, we do it. If the student needs a five-minute check-in prior to going to lunch to make sure the morning went well, then we do it. The key is that we are going to give students some action that they are responsible for taking. But we are not looking to add work, so all actions have to be agreed upon with the staff involved. Without this agreement and buy-in, the actionable step becomes a chore rather than a support.

## Explicitly Teach Expectations

A student most likely ends up in your restriction because of an expectation not being followed. Going back to our previous thought, students do not follow expectations because they do not understand them, or they need more practice. If the student has acted out for attention or to avoid something, that would still be in the way of them demonstrating understanding of an expectation. To truly make a restriction a learning opportunity, take time to teach or reteach the expectations.

This is not a simple task. If you are envisioning posting the expectations for lunch or the classroom on the board and having students write them out with an example, do not expect very much learning to take place. Draw on your own inspiration; mine has always been Mr. Miyagi, who helps me stay creative. Truthfully, we want to teach the expectations with modeling.

In order to demonstrate that students understand a topic in class, we most likely want them to be able to explain it, model it, and then teach it to another person. You may slightly disagree, but we feel if students can do those three things, they really have mastery of a topic. The expectations of the building should be approached in a similar fashion. We take time during restriction to let students discuss expectations, even if that means students telling us how stupid or wrong the expectations are. (Hint: students are really insightful and typically have a great understanding of why we have rules, but that does not mean they understand how to follow them). From this conversation, you are gaining the chance to explain how the expectations really work. Something we have all been guilty of is teaching an expectation and hoping most kids understand it rather than making sure everyone truly gets it. With the smaller audience and no academic material hanging over your head, you can have a thorough conversation about what the expectation entails.

Now it is time to model it. A tactic we really like is having the staff member take on the role of student to illustrate appropriate and inappropriate actions. This should be fun—get into character and give the students a good show so they can clearly point out the good and bad. When kids can point out the expectations to you as you perform, encourage them to model with each other. We say *encourage* because not all students will like this activity. However, the importance of modeling by the student is that it provides practice.

## Leave the Door Open

You have put into action a solid framework to support students. They have an opportunity to truly understand what is expected of them in your building. Students can help themselves get situated academically. Students have reflected and communicated their feelings in a way that can help. There has been real opportunity to get to know the students as individuals, and hopefully create a positive relationship. The key to sustaining that success is leaving the door open for students to gain additional assistance. Remember to encourage the students and talk with them outside of class whenever possible. If a student has a willingness to gain more support, we need to provide it. Let the student check in, or ask the other teachers about him or her so you can keep the dialogue going. Refresh the students on expectations now and then—not to dictate to them, but to make it clear they are not in it alone.

A huge consideration in taking these steps is time. Depending on the level of restriction you are using, you will have to change your action plan in creating these learning opportunities. In my building, we have after-school detention, lunch detention, restriction room, club time, and in-school suspension. When we are utilizing R.E.S.U.L.T.S. in a one-hour after-school detention or thirty-minute lunch detention, we are breaking up the steps over days or condensing our focus. If we are working with the student for one hour due to a single, isolated incident, we want to focus on reflecting and checking the understanding of expectations. These two things will best equip the student moving forward. In order to be thorough in our supportive situation, we are going to access students' grades so they know we are here to help.

When a student has more time in restriction, possibly 2–3 hours of restriction from a special school activity, we can think of the steps as learning targets we want to move through at a logical pace and order that works for us. With the additional time, we always consider how much academic work we can do during that time, if it will help start a trend of success for the students. The conversation and activities we want to do can be worked around schoolwork. There is no reason to be tied to any order of the steps, but we will say that in the end that door has to remain open. Finish your time together on a positive note.

In-school suspension and a situation where a student is spending a whole week in detention provides a rare and great opportunity. When a student is being held out of instruction for the entire school day, we can work through the steps of R.E.S.U.L.T.S. with fidelity. Allow the focus of the day to be making sure all academic support that can be offered is provided. Secondly, focus on the reflection of the student and provide an opportunity for the student to discuss the situation and show growth in understanding how to be successful. We want to make sure that the student leaves in-school suspension better equipped to manage the school day. This includes everything from organizing materials to learning how to ask for help effectively. The full week of detention is the same process over a course of days. Academically, we always want to help the student. One day we can focus on setting academic goals and organizing our action plan. The next day can be all about reflection on the situation that took place. There is no reason to feel tied to any specific structure; be flexible and use the framework within your own personal strengths.

# CHAPTER NINE
# Reinforcing Behaviors: Don't Buy the Candy Bar

## KRISTA

Anyone who is a parent has most likely experienced the dreaded checkout aisle that is lined with candy and toys. If you are not a parent, you have probably witnessed children being told they could not have a candy bar while in the checkout aisle. Every young child is going to want everything in the aisle, and after being told no, the child is probably going to communicate displeasure by engaging in a temper tantrum. Now, the adult's response—to give in and "buy the candy bar" or stand his or her ground and stick with the original "no" response—essentially reinforces the bad behavior or teaches the child that a tantrum is not going to result in getting what he or she wants.

Days before writing this chapter, I watched this play out right in front of me when checking out at a craft store. A six- or seven-year-old little girl wanted a toy, and the mother said she could not have it. The father then put it back on the shelf and walked away; maybe he anticipated that this was not going to end well and didn't want to be a part of what was about to ensue. The little girl went over to the shelf, got the toy, and walked back to her mother. The mom explained that if she got it now, it would be one less thing she could get for Christmas, and it would be more fun to get it in her stocking. The girl persisted, and the mother finally gave up. She stopped bargaining with the girl and did not say anything else but allowed her daughter to put the toy up on the counter and ended up buying it.

The girl learned, *if I keep pestering my parents, they will tire out and I will get what I want.* Some scenarios, especially when younger children are involved, include screaming, yelling, and whining. It is easy to judge when watching these situations take place, but put yourself in the parent's shoes. You can literally feel everyone's eyes on you, "judging" you, rolling their eyes, wishing you would just make your kid be quiet. The easiest and quickest thing to do to stop the tantrum is to "buy the candy bar," even though you said no and you really do not want your child to have it.

### Reinforcing Bad Behavior: "Buying the Candybar"

1. Child asks for candy in the checkout aisle of the grocery store.
2. Parent says no.
3. Child has a tantrum.
4. Parent is embarrassed, people are looking, rolling their eyes and may be commenting on the child's behavior.
5. Parent gives child the candy to stop the screaming even though it reinforces the bad behavior.

As parents and as educators, sometimes we cave and "buy the candy bar" because it is the fastest way to get the challenging behavior to stop. We need to remember that, at times, we have to endure "short-term pain for long-term gain." There are absolutely times when we need to do whatever we can in order to help a child come out of crisis when there is an imminent threat of danger to the child or others, but most times it is best to wait out the situation and try to help students work through the moment by providing other choices, giving the child time and space to calm down, and/or reminding the child of the strategies he or she has been taught. This may not be very pleasant for anyone, but it is a great learning opportunity that ensures we refrain from reinforcing poor behavior.

Providing an effective response or consequence for poor behavior may be highly inconvenient and could be a lengthy process, but in the long run it will save time because the child did not learn, *if I do this, they will give me what I want.*

We have found that if we really want to change a student's behavior, we need to change our own behavior. We have begun to implement a push-in support model when called to a classroom where a student is being highly disruptive.

> *... if we really want to change a student's behavior, we need to change our own behavior.*

Teachers are expected to handle typical classroom management issues. A call to the office is reserved for highly disruptive or dangerous situations. When an administrator is called, we go to the room and take over the supervision and teaching of the class. The teacher works with the disruptive student, preferably in the classroom. At times the teacher may need to take the student for a walk or to the wellness/sensory room.

If the first scenario is not an option for one reason or another, such as the student needing a new person to interact with, the administrator will attend to the student in the classroom while the teacher continues to teach the rest of the class. As with the first scenario, there may be a need for the administrator to take the student for a walk or to the wellness and sensory room, and then return the student to the classroom as soon as he or she is in an educable state again.

In situations when the child is a danger to him- or herself or others, the administrator will attempt to remove the child from the room or remove the other students from the room and begin de-escalation strategies.

We go through this process in order to support the teacher's authority and to encourage the relationship between the teacher and the student in crisis. If an administrator comes in and the first action he or she takes is to remove the child from the classroom, then we bought the candy bar! That is reinforcing bad behavior. Yes, we might seem like "the hero" in the moment by getting the student to leave the room and giving the teacher and the rest of the class a break from the situation, but we didn't fix anything. We will eventually bring the same child making poor choices back to the same class, and the child will most likely engage in the same behavior again.

Also, by taking the child out of the room, we completely undermine the teacher's authority in the classroom. It sends the message that the teacher cannot handle the situation and does not need to be listened to. We also do not want to diminish the relationship between the teacher and the student. Having the teacher work with the student provides the opportunity for them to work together to problem-solve the situation and develop or strengthen a positive relationship.

It is very important to support teachers with students who are being highly disruptive or in crisis, but it is equally important to not "buy the candy bar" and stay strong so that we can achieve long-term gain.

# CHAPTER TEN
# Meeting Social and Emotional Needs: A Menu of Skills

**JON**

Even as adults we can struggle to understand what we really need emotionally. In the same line of thinking, we often struggle to understand what we need to be self-aware or socially capable. Yet we expect middle-school students to innately understand these concepts. Part of our approach in the classroom and through intervention has to be identifying and growing necessary skills related to the social and emotional needs of students.

In order to effectively help students understand these needs, we separate them into two distinct groups. We label one group of skills as "interpersonal skills," which relate to a person's social awareness. Interpersonal skills are necessary for students to interact and manage relationships. Think of these skills as the student's ability to participate in his or her environment while being mindful of other people's needs.

The second group of skills we label as "personal motivations," which relate to a student's internal motivation and self-directedness. These skills are meant to encompass a student's work ethic and ability to persevere, be flexible, and be motivated to learn. We consider these skills to be intrinsic, meaning the social setting is only a factor that could affect motivation. We truly must focus our thinking on keeping these skills as a student's choice to grow with our support.

To effectively address both sets of skills, students must be aware of what skills they are addressing. In order to be effective in providing for social and emotional needs in conjunction with curriculum, we consider multiple strategies.

We do not always consider addressing social and emotional needs as an exercise separate from content.

We embed the tactics for addressing these skills within out content planning. Our assessments can have a focus area of skills to make sure we are addressing the social and emotional growth of our students. Without our knowledge, we are requiring these important skills as part of our planned activities. Now we are planning to be intentional in identifying what skills we are addressing.

### Consider building social and emotional skills into part of your routine.

Students love routine and appreciate the comfort in knowing what to expect in class. Empower them to interact with social and emotional skills as part of what you typically do through unit planning. Perhaps it works best for you to have a social and emotional skills warm-up regularly in class. Students could also have regularly scheduled reflections of these skills through the process of content. Giving up a minimal amount of instructional time regularly helps you as the teacher know students are having their social and emotional needs addressed.

### Incorporate meaningful feedback procedures.

If we are making it a point to have students interact with these important skills in an effort to grow, then all students need meaningful feedback. For the willing teacher, we provide a skills report that provides a separate grade on assessments in relation to the student's effective use of self-awareness and social responsibility. The purpose of the feedback is not just to let students know where they stand, but also to develop intervention plans for helping individual students grow their skills.

When we look to grow these skills for students, we must utilize a trickle-up approach. Students must have the opportunity to learn what these skills are at the elementary level. This will increase the effectiveness of strategies and intervention later in the student's academic career. A large issue we see at the middle level is students' lack understanding of how their actions impact others and how their emotions dictate their actions. With more social and emotional skills education at the primary level, students will become familiar with the terminology of the skills.

The trickle-up approach also builds a better opportunity to shift the focus at the middle level to be more reflective and student driven. While in the primary grades, we want to introduce the concept of students' own interpersonal skills and personal motivations; by the middle level, we want students to have the ability to reflect on their learning. Students will be able to identify what skills they address and how specifically they address them.

In the Social and Emotional Needs chart, we break down each list of skills into functional definitions to keep in mind, along with a working example of how you could address the skill within the content of your class. These are only ideas to help you brainstorm and make the addressing of social and emotional skills your own.

Keep in mind that we have not developed the full list of possibilities. The number of interpersonal skills to address could include overlap with personal motivations and unique skills we have not identified here. The important aspect of this concept is that we are expecting students to utilize a number of these skills, but not specifically addressing how to use them.

## R.E.S.U.L.T.S.

## Social and Emotional Needs: Interpersonal Needs

| Interpersonal Skill | Description | Functional Example |
|---|---|---|
| Social awareness | Ability to react and interact appropriately | Class debate: responding to different views |
| Relationship skills | Working collaboratively, handling conflict, managing emotions | Creating an argument for utilizing company resources in a specific way |
| Compassion | Care and concern for others | Create a list of things to do to show kindness for others |
| Ability to accept and learn from feedback | Seeing feedback as an opportunity for growth | Student conferences on a writing assignment |
| Cooperative problem solving | Recognizing the strengths of yourself and others to find solutions | Lab activity where the teacher changes rules to increase difficulty |
| Communication | Effective exchange of information | Corresponding with another class working on the same material |
| Acting as a team player | Accepting a role to contribute toward a goal | One product per group with a time constraint |
| Active listening | Receiving information to understand and engage | Developing questions in response to information: video, lecture, etc. |
| Leadership | Delegate duties, organize plans, make decisions | Math class, TEAM Huddle, delegate and fill roles |

The personal motivations in the table below are broken down in the same way. We want to show how students can grow their intrinsic motivation.

## Social and Emotional Needs: Personal Motivations

| Personal Motivations | Description | Functional Example |
|---|---|---|
| Self-awareness | Understanding your own emotions | Responding to an emotional video |
| Self-management | Controlling our reactions | Class debate activity |
| Self-confidence | Belief in your own capabilities | Choosing a method of presentation |
| Respectful decision making | Considering the well-being of self and others, evaluating consequences of own actions | Constructing historical interactions among people (identifying consequences of their actions) |
| Time management | Prioritizing tasks | Long-term assignments with deadlines and planned student work days |
| Work ethic | Recognizing the benefits of working hard | Reading/study logs, seeing positive outcomes from doing outside work |
| Flexibility/adaptability | Accepting what is out of our control | Teacher changing the rules to add difficulty |
| Resiliency | Emotional stability through challenges | Being given a new math concept to investigate without direction |
| Perseverance | Putting forth effort despite difficulty | Investigate an activity where your first solution does not work or is not right |

## R.E.S.U.L.T.S.

Don't limit yourself to just this list. Students at the middle level are constantly growing their ability to be socially responsible. We use the breakdown within these charts to ensure we have strategies to help students control their own motivation. Possessing skills like time management, work ethic, and resiliency will be paramount as the demands of secondary education increase.

## CHAPTER ELEVEN
# Applying R.E.S.U.L.T.S. in the Classroom

### JON

We encourage teachers to not just view R.E.S.U.L.T.S. as an intervention plan for a smaller group of students who have demonstrated misunderstanding of the expectations or other negative behaviors. All teachers feel strongly about their abilities to manage the classroom. As professionals, we all take a great deal of care in creating our procedures and getting to know our students. When using R.E.S.U.L.T.S. as programming for your individual class periods or your homeroom, you adjust the action steps of each letter slightly. This is an adaptation we are suggesting—certainly there are other options of how to use the framework to better serve your purpose. Part of using R.E.S.U.L.T.S. is having the freedom to be creative for your students.

One piece of advice for using R.E.S.U.L.T.S. in the classroom is to be mindful of your consistency. In order to find value in using the framework, there needs to be logical organization to your process. Make sure to build a routine that works for you as the teacher, but also for your students as a team and as individuals. Also, as a disclaimer, you will have to commit yourself to sacrificing instructional time regularly in your planning.

We feel these adjustments to each part of R.E.S.U.L.T.S. allow you as the teacher to best support individual students and build great rapport with students. Utilizing the framework in this way allows for intervention, but also the consistent review of expectations. We feel students will appreciate the procedure and routine associated with this framework. Over the period of the school year, communication should improve as students are more willing to share and have a deeper connection as part of the team or class group.

### Review the Current Situation

As intervention for individual students, we consider reviewing the current situation an opportunity to open up the conversation with the student on what exactly has been going on. When utilizing R.E.S.U.L.T.S. in the classroom, we can still use it as a response to isolated incidents that may require intervention. A teacher wanting to take on providing that intervention for the student is excellent. However, we can consider two other uses of "review the situation." One is as a tool for whole-class accountability. This would be an opportunity to discuss how the class transitions, or if there is an area of class in which students have been struggling. An area we have found value in is how the teacher addresses the class in regard to behavior for a guest teacher. This is one small part of unifying a class as a team or small community. The second use lies in reviewing the current situation as a source of gaining feedback from your class. You can open up the floor for students to express what they like, what they dislike, or what they may just have questions about. When you continue to take the time to do this step, the conversation will increase. Students always shock us with their insightfulness in regard to all things school related.

### Evaluate Progress

The concept of this step does not have to change much within the classroom. Rather than providing it to only those students who have shown a need, now you are making it part of your classroom procedure. Within this step is the time to utilize regularly scheduled academic check-in days where students will have the opportunity, as part of your class, to know their grades and consider what assignments they have not been finishing. Also, it allows the teacher to monitor growth among students both academically and behaviorally. This is the step where we take the student who was not completing any in-class assignments at the start of the quarter and now is finishing half the work in a timely manner, and we celebrate that growth. We are providing students a time-out from content to discuss growth.

From a behavioral standpoint, evaluating progress in the classroom is a decision controlled by the teacher. In a sense, students can be given an opportunity to measure their improvement. When a behavior of concern is present, and immediate intervention does not correct the behavior, students need an opportunity to investigate what is going on. As the behavior continues, evaluating progress is relationship based, trying to navigate what is going on when the student enters your room and how you can help. Then, we want to reward growth again. If the student identifies the trigger or can explain how he or she made a decision to avoid a negative behavior, we reward immediately in some simple way (high five, handshake, or your own twist that fits your personality).

## Self-Assess

As part of your classroom routines, it is a great step to have periodical built-in opportunities for reflection. This is not a time for the teacher to tell students what they have been doing. This is a student-led activity where they have to discuss what they could have done differently, their successes, and their failures. *Periodical* can mean many things and bring a different level of comfort for each teacher. The opportunity to self-assess needs to be frequent enough that the students feel the impact of trying to apply what they have learned about themselves. Personally, I like the thought of a monthly self-assessment that works well with my assessment plan of a given unit or with the building calendar. It takes more time to consider these things when planning ahead, but it pays off as students grow.

## Utilize Time Wisely

In order to utilize time wisely in the classroom setting, we want to provide students with meaningful opportunities to prepare themselves for learning. Students do not come to school without finished homework or unprepared for a test on purpose. Also, students do not want to make their lives more difficult by choice; we have to consider circumstances and what skills students are coming to school with.

When we talk about using time wisely, we first focus on the academic aspects. In your classroom, you can provide opportunities for students to organize parallel with your content. In my classroom, I have always had students keep portfolios of their different demonstrations of learning. Part of our cycle routine was to do housekeeping days; the portfolio always gave a good reason for housekeeping. As part of my long-term planning, I would structure housekeeping days as part of differentiated learning centers. Students would have to go through a checklist of housekeeping items, including a study schedule, planner check, etc., while I was navigating the room and checking in at a reteaching station, an enrichment station, and usually some sort of review station. Students would rotate through so everyone would have the opportunity to build a time plan, and I was provided a great opportunity to interact and check in with students. Many of you most likely have a similar practice; we are suggesting making it part of your weekly cycle or unit planning.

Now, to speak about behavioral aspects of using time wisely, we shift our focus to empowering students to help themselves. In a restriction setting, students would focus on using time wisely by considering where they need to grow and what strategies could help them get there. We focus utilizing time on practices that help students stay ready to learn. As part of your class, you can institute regularly scheduled moments of mindfulness or work on some basic meditation practices. Keep in mind that these are more sacrifices to your instructional time, but they are front-loaded. Students will need to be taught these strategies and activities along with your other procedures and expectations. As the school year moves forward, you can make decisions about utilizing time more frequently or less frequently. Also, you can identify an intervention group of students, and take utilizing time wisely to a new level of relationship building. Take advantage of having students in a smaller setting, outside of instructional time, to work on the functions of being a student in your class.

## Lose the Clutter

In order to lose the clutter academically, get rid of what you do not need. Take time to remove those distractions regularly, in correlation with the housekeeping method discussed in "Utilizing Time Wisely." One strategy we always talk about is not liking messiness, so we convince the students to pitch what they do not need as a way to save us from our own neurosis. What we are really doing is taking time during class to let kids identify what they need or do not need. This is different from a traditional notebook check because it is really more of a lifeline to once again build a relationship.

Maybe it works better for you to identify the student who really needs additional help, and take the initiative to be a "clutter buddy." This physical clutter is a safe space for kids; they do not mind talking through it. What lies underneath the physical clutter requires a special relationship to get through.

Losing the clutter from an emotional standpoint requires knowing our students exceptionally well. Building trust is one part of getting to this point of students opening up about the barriers to their learning. Take time early in the year to not only work in activities to get to know your students, but also make it a point to follow up with them. As the year progresses, give opportunities to let students speak about what is bothering them. If you do the job of making your classroom a positive climate and safe space, students will open up. You as an educator can facilitate the conversation about what bothers students at your school. Once you have identified an area in which you can help a student, provide the personal intervention.

At this moment, you may be asking, "How and when do I do that?" I do not have all the answers, but what has worked for me is making it relate to my lesson and using a conversation activity as part of my own activating strategy. My personal favorite is, "What grinds my gears?" Essentially, we are using questioning to allow students to complain about things in school. It takes some fancy footwork to keep it appropriate and provide damage control, but it addresses the human aspect of education. Kids need a safe chance to talk. These conversations provide us little hints and triggers to find out more about students who need help but are not ready to ask for it. Consider the step of losing clutter as one support provided in the whole program of R.E.S.U.L.T.S.

## Take the Initiative

This is the crucial step where we make sure students have a handle on the who, where, and how for gaining support. An important aspect of middle level education, in our opinion, is growing students' ability to advocate for themselves. Within your classroom you can take time to review how students ask for help in your class, specifically how they access the supports you provide. This can include reviewing how to sign up for after-school, lunch, or intervention period help in your class. Also, you can review the crucial skill of asking a meaningful question. This helps students be able to tell you what they do not understand, rather than telling you, "I don't get it." By routinely sacrificing instructional time, you can better prepare students to ask for help, which will help you gain instruction time in the long run.

Do not think of just the domain of your individual classroom. Within your class, you can continue to grow students' social and emotional learning skills. Students can be taught how to access supports within the building. As a classroom teacher, take the time to review and check for students' understanding of how the communication between teachers and other points of support (counselors, psychologists, therapists, the principal, etc.) works. Maybe the student is not comfortable coming forward when he or she needs help. We should all be dedicated to not missing an opportunity to help a student feel more comfortable asking for help. In our experience, we often say, "If we only knew more, we could have helped." The only way to get past that issue is to constantly build in opportunities to grow our relationships with students and teach the skills of self-advocacy.

## Set Goals

Academically, when a student consistently struggles with the same thing, what do we do? We build some sort of action plan and we set a goal, something tangible that students can reach for. Is there any reason to not apply the same mindset to behavior? A first step to take is teaching a lesson on how to set a goal, focusing on how to make it measurable and attainable. Also, make sure it is something tangible in the sense that students can see the difference that meeting the goal creates.

If a student has continued to struggle with a specific behavior or procedure within your classroom, take the time to address it. Use R.E.S.U.L.T.S. as a plan to determine what specifically you want to change. You can cycle this through as a part of your planning that you always dedicate to R.E.S.U.L.T.S., or you can come together with the student another time (lunch, after school, etc.). An important part of setting goals is not just saying, "You will do this by this date." That practice is not actionable enough. What students need is to identify what they want to change, and then be provided an opportunity to work with you as the adult to develop action steps to get there. Your role as the teacher is to be the sponsor of that goal; the student can come to you, but you must seek out the student to check on the goal.

The other important part of setting goals as part of R.E.S.U.L.T.S. is attaching a time frame. It is crucial to help students build that structure of wanting to show improvement over a certain amount of time. For you as the educator, the time frame is what allows you to organize yourself as to how you will support that student in that window of time. Together, you and the student will hold each other accountable for action steps.

Now for the fun part of setting goals as part of R.E.S.U.L.T.S. in the classroom: rewarding! If you are setting a goal to work on countering a recurring behavior, you and the student both need a time to celebrate success. Sure, you will always commend the student for positive behavior immediately, but there is more. Students will respond to your excitement about the opportunity to celebrate success. Make sure to keep your voice positive and always be pumping the student up so that the student knows you will get there together.

R.E.S.U.L.T.S. can seem like a daunting task to regularly take on within the classroom. Always keep in mind that there is no wrong way to do the steps, and no rule about when to do each step. We propose regularly setting aside time in your planning to address different components of R.E.S.U.L.T.S.

# CHAPTER TWELVE
# Focus on Growth

### JON

If we really consider the standard responses to negative behavior, are we setting students up for success? We struggle to find anything in traditional discipline that breaks the cycle of negative behavior. More often, traditional consequences continue a pattern of negative behavior or add an additional layer to a preexisting issue. Even when we improve traditional consequences with the use of reflection or giving students an opportunity to review expectations, we are still not finding success for that individual student. If we want to get serious about supporting that one student who desperately needs it, then we have to focus on the growth beyond academics.

We want to be clear: focusing on growth does not mean creating fake success to make students feel good. What we are pushing here is far different. Do not think of faking success; think of differentiating, just like instruction, to allow the student an opportunity to have success. When a difficult student acts out, we are disciplining the student from the administrative level to support the teacher and allow instruction to continue. However, we are doing ourselves a disservice because administrators are not in your classroom, their instruction was not interrupted, and their relationship with the student was most likely not even affected. That is why the teachers adapting to and focusing on growth in areas of behavior is so key—it avoids the negative cycle of reactionary discipline.

So, time for big questions. Where do we do it? How do we do it?

The simple question is *where* we do it, because we practice growing everywhere all the time. My analogy for this is my feeble attempts at using a pogo stick. I tried for about five minutes, only able to bounce the pogo stick one time until, finally, I managed to bounce twice. Immediately, my brother exclaimed, in all of his wisdom, "Hey, two is better than one!" That seems like just a logical response. However, I can tell you that bouncing twice was not enough for me to keep going—the difference was the validation from my brother stating the simple fact that two times was an improvement. Focusing on growth is a culture, a way of life for us. We refuse to accept that students come to school wanting to fail; it goes against human nature. Even if the behavior screams that the student wants to get worse, it is all just a front hiding a lack of belief in his or her own ability to grow.

In order to answer the how, we consider what conventions already exist in school, and we make a decision to be very intentional in the way we conduct our day. That means getting rid of phrases that carry any negative connotation. If a kid comes to your class two minutes late every day and then shows up only one minute late, avoid the urge to make a joke about it or use the same line about being on time. Instead, consider the opportunity in front of you, and thank the student for coming to class earlier, saying you plan to keep making your class better so he or she wants to be there on time every day. You see, focusing on growth becomes easier the first time we make a connection and see a student recognize his or her own growth. Simply, we need to engage with students, point out victories, and share ownership over getting better.

To strategize, consider the following areas:

## Celebrations

There is a tactic to use when having celebrations. Even the smallest of successes deserves a celebration, but every kid is different. This leaves two options.

One, have a great relationship with all your kids so that your standard style of celebration over what some may consider trivial things is always well received and expected. Two, individualize and publicly praise the students who want it and quietly and personally praise the students who need it, but not on a grand scale. Either way, students have to know you mean it; the excitement or pride has to be real.

Students benefit from celebrations by receiving validation and attention. We like to keep in mind that all students need attention, some more than others. Celebrations are a form of having control over that need for attention. If a student improves a grade or increases participation, we must remove any focus from the standard we try to fit all students into and recognize that individual student taking a step forward.

## Not Quite Yet... But We'll Get There

Dr. Carol Dweck is a psychologist at Stanford University and is famous for her work on motivation. In the TED Talk "The Power of Believing that You Can Improve,"[1] she talks about the wildly popular mantra in schools everywhere: "The Power of Yet." The power of yet may seem like a simple concept, but personally, it took me years of coaching and teaching until I realized it was a gold mine. Consider the difference between these two statements:

"Hey, it's okay that you didn't make it."

"Hey, we just aren't there *yet*."

The first statement is supportive, telling a student it is okay. There is even proof that you care because you are taking into consideration that the student is most likely frustrated. One major problem with it, though, is that you just let the student accept the failure and inadvertently told the student you are not a team.

The second statement is powerful in many ways. First is the word *we*. The word *we* becomes the most important word because it makes it very clear to

---

[1] Dweck, Carol. "The Power of Believing that You Can Improve." https://www.ted.com/talks/carol_dweck_the_power_of_believing_that_you_can_improve?language=en.

the student that he or she is not in this alone. Even if you have to use that phrase a hundred times, it is still *we*. As long as you back it up with trying, eventually that student is going to believe that *we* is a real thing. Secondly, the statement is open-ended. If every time I ever failed, someone told me we just were not there *yet*, I would have taken a million more risks and tried a million times harder. Even if students do not believe they can truly do it, the word *yet* makes them think about what *yet* can really mean. The second phrase evokes a much more meaningful conversation that can be about action. Most importantly, the word *yet* shows no acceptance of failure.

## Positive Language

There are a million (okay, maybe not a million) things to like about the word *failure*. The words *can't*, *won't*, and *not* are bad words that we consider negative language. *Failure*, though, is not a bad word because failure is a real thing. Positive language is all about the ownership we take in failure. Students have to experience setbacks and challenges; they have to fail to a certain extent so they can learn to be resilient. Failure can be a key to building a student's grit, the ability to desire more. Our positive language is finding a way to create parameters for success.

Here is an example. A student comes into your class. The student has studied for an assessment and is confident of doing well. You grade the assessment, and the student does not do well. The negative language we fall into is saying that the student must not have studied correctly or missed an important part of the material. The student already has the grade and knows something went wrong, so why do we focus on that? Instead, consider a conversation that focuses on the positive. This student made the great choice to prepare for the exam, and had the confidence to come into your classroom and give her best effort. That needs to be the focus. "Hey, so it did not go well, but I am proud of you for studying and caring enough to give that effort." Now you can dive into what was lost in translation and find some solutions. Positive language can be so much more actionable than a negative voice.

Focusing on positive language changes the narrative for the student and allows the student to focus on the learning that took place through the failure. It is not okay to say a student does not get it or is not willing. Truthfully, we get a little sick to our stomachs every time we hear that phrase in a parent meeting or a student conference. A student being unwilling or not getting it is a "we" problem; that is our job. Eliminate that thought process from your brain and focus on your own growth as an educator because that is what our kids need and deserve.

## Tailor Your Steps to Focus on Growth

Whether you are working through the steps of R.E.S.U.L.T.S. or trying to get students to concept mastery, take control of the parameters for individual students. To do this, we attach our areas of growth to manageable goals. This means specific areas and actions through which students can feel the difference. We have all been in a situation where we think students are completely in sync with what we are teaching, only to find out something got lost in translation. We feel this is because knowledge can be abstract and difficult to make tangible. Take the time to individualize for students so they know the steps to take to attain a goal.

## R.E.S.U.L.T.S.
## Improving the Situation is a Process

There is a great benefit to considering that each letter of R.E.S.U.L.T.S. can be treated as a separate learning opportunity and mode of practice. Perhaps for an individual student, one letter of R.E.S.U.L.T.S. requires the most practice but will bring about the best outcomes. If the goal of any intervention program is to increase student success, then we have to consider that improvement is a process.

If a student is unable to evaluate progress or communicate what the situation really is, do we stop trying to help? Of course not! We have to work around that barrier or remove some other barriers for the student. We want to avoid letting anyone believe that running a student through these seven activities equals an automatic fix. Gosh, it would be nice if that were the case, but we all know that's not how interventions work. This is why we stress the importance of focusing on growth.

Maybe a student is still making a similar mistake or resisting what seems like an easy positive choice. However, it is happening less frequently, or there is less tension with the teacher in a negative situation. As you work through R.E.S.U.L.T.S., this is the growth you will see. Students will latch onto the time you are taking to build a relationship. Eventually, they will open up and feel comfortable sharing what they need. Once we get to that point, growth can happen exponentially faster.

If we as educators, take the time to allow students to respond to the intervention R.E.S.U.L.T.S. provides, we show students patience and commitment. R.E.S.U.L.T.S. has the built-in conversation to allow students to grow without realizing it. We recognize students will fail, and possibly fail again, but even a small success can help those students find value in the process of R.E.S.U.L.T.S.

A good friend of mine often tells me that we are in the business of changing lives. If we consider that while using R.E.S.U.L.T.S., we have to remember the process may change one small behavior at a time, but it will eventually make a large impact on a student's life.

## Believing in Students

The concept of believing in students enough so that they can learn to believe in themselves appears in this book multiple times. It is intentional; it is that important. We encounter so many students who seem to carry the most confidence in the world. Frequently, those students fall into social groups where all students tend to be at risk or struggle academically, behaviorally, etc. These are the students who need an opportunity to grow and find direction. For this group, success is not found between the bells of your class period.

For many at-risk students, that sense of belonging does not exist in their school, except within a social group made up of students who also do not feel a worthwhile sense of belonging. I always see it as groups of students who want to do better, but nobody has the skills to lead their peers. Find these students and let them know you care and believe in them!

# CHAPTER THIRTEEN
# Family Buy-In and Support

## JON

Fostering positive relationships should not be limited to just our students during the school day. In the interest of student success, we should have cooperative relationships with parents and guardians. While there are many avenues to communicate with a student's family, it is important to have an approach that does not simply share negative feedback but creates shared accountability. Student success is our responsibility, so our communication with the parents has to clearly show we are seeking their support.

These conversations are not always easy, especially when we are met with negative or defensive parents. Every parent or guardian has the right to be heard, so allow the conversation to run its course so a partnership can be formed. If we are providing information about how we aim to help someone's son or daughter, we can overcome negativity.

We want to take time to reflect on how we have crafted our approach for communicating with parents and think of how we can shift our language to be positive and supportive at all times. Also, we want to take advantage of different avenues or opportunities to interact with parents.

## Evening School Events

Every year at the middle level we prepare ourselves for a back-to-school night. There are always unknowns attached to the open house that takes place early in the school year. Sometimes, we may not be aware of the background or possible issues with our students at the early point of the school year. Our suggestion is to spend your designated times to interact with parents talking about your communication plan. Make yourself clearly accessible, and encourage parents to reach out. Then, follow through on the different ways you explained that you would be in contact with them.

There are many other opportunities to interact with parents outside of back-to-school night. Take advantage of other times your administration brings parents into the building for events. If someone from your school is sharing information with your students' parents, volunteer to be present and allow for more accessibility and opportunities for quality conversation. This can include chaperoning for school events.

This approach is difficult; obviously you have a life outside of school that needs to be balanced. Within our schedules, there is a level of compromise that makes us available more than required. This accessibility shows a presence outside of the classroom and allows for situations where parents may be more comfortable communicating.

## Positive Voice

Remember that you are building a partnership, so it is not okay to tell a parent, "He won't do this" or, "She doesn't seem interested to ever do that." These are problems that we want all parties to share accountability for. Enter into the conversation with the parent loaded with factual information about strategies you have tried and how the student reacted. Make the conversation tell a story of where your journey has gone so far, and ask to share some ideas on what to try next. The most important aspect of the conversation has to be conveying your desire to find the best way to support the child.

## Keep Them Informed

Accessibility is very important to parents. Sometimes, for our most challenging students, we are struggling to keep that connection. We take it upon ourselves to provide communication in multiple ways. Showing a presence through the school website or social media forms a great connection with modern families. Also, take advantage of technology in order to send information home to parents often.

## Communicate Student Response to Results

While you are cycling students through the learning opportunities of R.E.S.U.L.T.S., inform parents of student responses to the provided intervention. This feedback to the parents can be specific in order to communicate what your next steps will be. By allowing parents to be informed and heard throughout this step, they feel shared ownership in the improvement of their child.

## Tangible Feedback

While conversation provides peace of mind about which activities you are completing with their child, parents appreciate tangible evidence of their student's work. Keep portfolios of student work through R.E.S.U.L.T.S. and utilize technology to share electronic work. We believe this step helps generate meaningful and productive conversation. *Tangible* means something parents can view and discuss with their children. Technology can eliminate any chance of items sent home with students not arriving for the parent. However, we want to note that if R.E.S.U.L.T.S. is bringing positive attention to the student at school and at home, sharing with parents should be easier through any means.

## CHAPTER FOURTEEN
# Self-Care and Emotional Wellness for Staff: We Are All Human

**KRISTA**

As educators, we make hundreds of decisions per day that affect others. We constantly worry about our students—usually at two o'clock in the morning when we should be sleeping. We stress ourselves out wondering if we are doing enough for others, if we are meeting the needs of all of our students, if we are doing everything to make our supervisors happy, if we are communicating enough so that our students' parents feel connected . . . and that's just about school. On top of that, we worry about our own families and friends and the personal and professional goals we have set for ourselves.

Due to our very busy lives, many times our own physical, mental, and emotional health is pushed to the back of the priority line. In reality, it needs to be front and center in order for us to be the best version of ourselves for ourselves and others. It is important to find the things that give you peace, bring you joy, and fill your cup. Then you must make time to give these things the proper attention.

We have all heard the sayings, "It's just a job," "Everyone is replaceable," and, "On their deathbed nobody wishes they spent more time at the office," but I do not buy into those adages when it comes to a career in education. To explain, we will borrow a line from our superintendent, "We aren't making

> *It is important to find the things that give you peace, bring you joy, and fill your cup.*

coffee pots here. We are dealing with human souls." Our work is so important, and it is not "just a job." Yes, people are replaced when they move on from a position or a district, but the lives they touched will forever carry the love, time, and effort that was given to them. And we are willing to bet there are many educators lying on their deathbeds who do wish they had more time to spend with the children and colleagues they gave so much to during their careers. It's not just a job—it is truly a lifestyle that requires so much from your mind and body and takes a toll on your emotions.

It is easier said than done, but ensuring that you make time to stay healthy will make you a better educator and participant in your life outside of school. Make a schedule, seek out accountability buddies, splurge on yourself when you are able, take time to reflect, and just "be."

Ways to take care of your body may include taking a walk around the hallways before school, working out at the gym or in your home, riding a stationary bike while watching your favorite show, practicing yoga, playing with students during recess, walking your dog, riding a bike, stretching, swimming, rock climbing, and hiking.

Mindfulness options you can utilize may include many of the same activities that are good for your body as well as breathing exercises, visualization, and meditation. There are countless apps and videos online to guide you through these activities. Doing things that relax and recharge you helps with your creativity and gives you the burst you need to get back to doing what you do best—educating students and being a good family member, friend, and colleague. When you are able, get a massage, travel, curl up and read a book, or sit and relax while you enjoy a cup of coffee or tea.

Reflecting at the end of the day is a great way to review the wonderful things that you have done as well as rethink how you may choose to do things differently next time. A colleague, whom I consider a stellar teacher, shared that he grades himself at the end of each day. He actually gives himself an A, B, C, D, or F for the day and jots down a note about why he scored himself that way. This is a person who brings his "A-game" each day, so we are sure that there are not too many days outside of the "A–B" range. It's the fact that he takes this time to reflect on his day and purposefully chooses to think about ways he can improve that says a lot and brings him closure to each day so that he may go into the next day renewed and ready to begin again.

A practice that my teachers are being asked to do this year is a quick entry in a reflection journal. The entry does not need to be long or in-depth. The value is in the time spent reflecting. Each entry looks like this:

Date: _____

1. Something I am grateful for today: _____

_____

2. Something I did today that I am proud of: _____

_____

3. Something I will improve upon next time: _____

_____

4. A kind act I performed, received, or witnessed: _____

_____

5. Any thoughts or ideas I do not want to forget: _____

_____

When new student teachers begin at my school, I hold an orientation breakfast for them and their cooperating teachers. One of the first things I share with them is the importance of self-care. I tell them that I wish it had not taken me fifteen-plus years to begin working on this. I wish that it had been part of my routine from the start of my career—maybe I would be better at it by now. I will keep trying!

## CHAPTER FIFTEEN
# Final Thoughts: How Will You Get R.E.S.U.L.T.S.?

In the dedication, we told you that you would meet a student who inspired us, lit the fire under us, and made it impossible for us to give up. This student is representative of many others who have touched our hearts and of the thousands of students who are near and dear to each of you.

There is no such thing as a magic wand that fixes every issue. No one is ever going to have all the powers and be able to—poof!—solve all of the problems or be able to erase the trauma, skill deficits, and struggles children have. No framework has all of the answers, but we will forever maintain that a plan and a person (or team of people, preferably) who will never give up is where the true magic lies.

We can never stop fighting to help kids realize the true treasures that they are and the limitless potential they possess. We need to make sure they know that if they have not figured out a way to meet with success yet, we will help them get there. We owe it to our students to teach them and give them opportunities to practice and experience the sweet feeling of success so that they may experience the pride that comes along with effort, drive, and a desire to reach their goals—goals they may never have dreamed they could achieve!

We will end by introducing you to one of our amazing former students, Samantha, who has taught us more about compassion, grit, and hard work than we could ever teach her.

## Thoughts from Samantha

Photo credit:
Crystal Alberta Photography

*My connection with Ms. Venza and Mr. Treese is something that I will always hold near to my heart. When tough things were going on they helped me to see past the moment and keep going. I knew I could always go to them, even when I got in trouble for stupid stuff. Although they may have been disappointed, they didn't shut me out, and they pushed me to be the best me that I could be.*

*I'm now a senior, but this connection began when I was in 8th grade. When I was struggling with something, I asked my teachers if I could go talk to Ms. Venza. I was always granted permission because they knew she was the one who could calm me down. Ms. Venza started a community service club called PEACE Crew, and she encouraged me to get involved. I met some of my closest friends there and had the opportunity to participate in activities that helped my community. We planted flowers, painted over graffiti in our town, held food drives and fund-raisers for important causes, and talked about important issues. She pushed me out of my comfort zone and I actually presented in front of a room of over one hundred people! People were actually listening to what I had to say! I got to talk to all of our teachers at an in-service about how to deal with students who act like I used to.*

*I learned how to be compassionate, to have empathy, and to believe in myself. I made some major changes in my life to help myself become more successful. I made the changes and I did the work, but Ms. Venza and Mr. Treese were there to encourage me every step of the way. I've gotten to do a lot of things, get involved in activities, and doors have opened for me because of their support of me.*

*I have kept in touch with Ms. Venza and Mr. Treese throughout my high school career. I will be graduating this year. They believe in me. I know they will always be in my corner. I can't wait to see their faces when I graduate later this year. They are "my people." Because of them I want to be somebody's person someday.*

This…is why we can never give up. To borrow a saying from a dear friend of ours, "When all else fails, just hug 'um." Sometimes this is where we need to start. Every day we can work on our relationships and connections with our students. Even on days when students aren't in an educable state due to past trauma, or are engaging in spiraling behaviors, we can always make sure they know we are on their side and here to help them. When students truly know and believe this, even on the not-so-great days, it makes it all the more possible for them to learn from us on the good days.

The smallest of gestures, things that we do not give a second thought, can make all the difference in the lives of our students. Helping kids become good human beings who positively contribute to the world is the greatest gift we can give them. Never underestimate your power as an educator—you are a life changer.

> *Helping kids become good human beings who positively contribute to the world is the greatest gift we can give them.*

## ABOUT THE AUTHORS
# Krista M. Venza and Jonathan R. Treese

### Krista Venza, M.Ed.

Krista is an educator, fierce advocate for what is best for students, believer in a balance between academics and social-emotional learning, community service organizer, presenter, author, learner, and promoter of kindness.

She is the principal of an elementary school with over 1,100 students grades kindergarten through third grade. She previously served as a middle school assistant principal and instructional support facilitator. She was also a ninth through twelfth grade emotional support special education teacher. Her goal for each day is that every student feels safe and welcome at school so that they are able to achieve their full potential as learners and contributing members of the community. She strives to create an atmosphere where teachers are able to use their instructional talents to inspire all students to learn and grow in a supportive, caring environment.

*Photo credit: Jack Venza*

Krista's Bachelor of Science in Education and certifications in elementary and special education are from Kutztown University, in Kutztown, Pennsylvania. Her Master's degree in Educational Leadership and K-12

R.E.S.U.L.T.S.

principal certification are from Immaculata University in Immaculata, Pennsylvania.

Krista enjoys spending time with her family and friends and keeping up with her sons and the many sporting, musical, and outreach events they are involved in.

Connect with Krista:
Twitter: @KristaVenza and @MrsVenza
Instagram: kristavenza
Facebook: /krista.venza

## Jonathan Treese, M.Ed.

*Photo Credit:
Cyrstal Alberta Photography*

Jonathan is an educator who has dedicated himself to optimizing positive relationships and developing action steps for student intervention. Over the course of his career, Jonathan has focused on at-risk youth in multiple settings. In recent years, Jon has taken pride in presenting his ideals and developing programming to help better serve the needs of individual students.

Jonathan's career has moved into administration, and he is currently serving as Dean of Students at a Pennsylvania middle school. Prior to being Dean of Students, he taught social studies at the middle and high school levels.

A passion for Jon is coaching high school basketball. His values as an educator carry over in his attempt to use basketball as a vehicle to help student athletes be successful in their preparation for life.

Jonathan obtained his Bachelor's Degree in History from Lebanon Valley College and his teaching certification through Lycoming College, both located in Pennsylvania. He has recently finished a Master's Degree in Educational Development and Strategies through Wilkes University, the same school where he is currently working on his Principal Certification Program.

In his time outside of education, Jon enjoys traveling and enjoying new experiences with his family. He is an avid sports fan who takes advantage of every opportunity to read about coaching philosophy and take in any sporting event.

Connect with Jon:
Twitter: @jt2510
Instagram: treesejon
Facebook: /jon.treese

*We would like to give a huge shout out to the fantastic educators we work with, admire, and value. Your dedication to our students is second to none and we are honored to have the opportunity to work with you.*
*A special thank you to the following people who, just by being awesome, provided us with quotes, stories, and teaching strategies to share in our book.*

**Dr. Joseph Macharola**
**Mr. Matt Coldren**
**Mr. Kriss Bellanca**
**Mr. Zach Milch**